Life with an Electric Car

Other Books by Noel Perrin

A Passport Secretly Green

Dr. Bowdler's Legacy

Vermont in All Weathers

Amateur Sugar Maker

First Person Rural

Giving Up the Gun

Second Person Rural

Third Person Rural

A Reader's Delight

A Noel Perrin Sampler

Last Person Rural

Life with an Electric Car

Noel Perrin

SIERRA CLUB BOOKS

San Francisco

For Rodney Palmer, longtime owner of Palmer's Garage, Thetford Center; Bob Evans and Bob Watson of Huggett's Garage, East Thetford; John Poor of Thetford Auto; Harold Clough of Railroad Street Mobil, St. Johnsbury: Vermont mechanics all. And for Darshan Bhatia, Indian engineer and member of the Dartmouth Solar Racing Team. These men have supplied the expertise that kept any vehicle I owned going, for the last thirty years and more.

The Sierra Club, founded in 1892 by John Muir, has devoted itself to the study and protection of the earth's scenic and ecological resources—mountains, wetlands, woodlands, wild shores and rivers, deserts and plains. The publishing program of the Sierra Club offers books to the public as a nonprofit educational service in the hope that they may enlarge the public's understanding of the Club's basic concerns. The point of view expressed in each book, however, does not necessarily represent that of the Club. The Sierra Club has some sixty chapters coast to coast, in Canada, Hawaii, and Alaska. For information about how you may participate in its programs to preserve wilderness and the quality of life, please address inquiries to Sierra Club, 730 Polk Street, San Francisco, CA 94109.

Published by arrangement with W. W. Norton & Company, Inc.

LIBRARY OF CONGRESS CATALOGING IN PUBLICATION DATA
Perrin, Noel.
   [Solo]
   Life with an electric car / Noel Perrin.
      p.   cm.
   Originally pub.: Solo. New York : Norton, 1992.
   ISBN 0-87156-497-1
   1. Automobiles, Electric.   2. Perrin, Noel—Journeys.
   3. Automobiles, Electric—United States—History.   I. Title.
   TL220.P38   1994
   629.25'02—dc20   94-6309

Production by Robin Rockey • Cover design by Amy Evans

Printed in the United States of America on acid-free paper containing a minimum of 50% recovered waste paper, of which at least 10% of the fiber content is post-consumer waste.

10   9   8   7   6   5   4   3   2   1

NOTE TO THE
PAPERBACK EDITION

THIS BOOK originally came out in 1992. A lot has changed in the world of electric cars since then. I've therefore added three new chapters at the end, and also revised the list of places where you can buy an electric vehicle. In 1992 I knew of five companies producing them: two in California, two in Florida, and one in Massachusetts. I now know of seventeen: six in California, and the other eleven pretty well spread around the United States. Two hundred percent growth in two years isn't bad.

One other note. I have not included any of the Big Three on the list. One is not yet selling electric vehicles, and the other two are selling very small quantities, at prices more suitable for buying a new house than for buying a car.

All is not lost in Detroit, however. Robert Stempel, the immediate past chairman of GM (he figures later in this book), is in the process of forming an electric car company right now. That's only one of many reasons I think the next list will be longer still.

Noel Perrin
February 1994

CONTENTS

PROLOGUE

THE SCENE is a classroom at Dartmouth College. The time is the winter of 1990. Forty-six students and a professor are in the room; together they constitute the course called Environmental Studies 1.

This week they have all been reading John McPhee's book *Encounters with the Archdruid,* and now they're discussing the central character. He is David Brower, savior of the Grand Canyon, one-time executive director of the Sierra Club.

The professor, though he admires Brower, can't resist a wisecrack. Brower is currently in the habit of taking jet airplanes around the United States in order to give lectures on, among other things, energy conservation. The professor says it would be a little more consistent if he were to ride a mule. "He would certainly give fewer speeches that way," the professor concedes. "But he would be in a much stronger moral position."

Instantly one of the seniors in the class raises her hand. "Can I ask you a personal question?" she says.

The professor hesitates. "Well, if it's not *too* personal."

"I understand you live on a farm over in Vermont."

"That's true."

"How far from the college are you?"

"Thirteen miles." He is beginning to see this coming.

"So, how did you get into Hanover this morning to teach this class?"

She has caught him fair and square. "I drove in, in my gas-guzzling, air-polluting farm truck," he admits. The class roars with laughter.

After class, another senior, worried that the professor may have got his feelings hurt, lingers for a minute. "I just wanted to tell you," he says, "that Alison isn't in perfect moral shape, either. She has her mom's station wagon up here this term. It doesn't get much rest.

9

She's been known to drive to Boston and back the same day. In fact," he says, generously offering up his own moral position, "I usually go with her."

I was that professor. Alison was one of my best students. I don't mind looking foolish in class, and a good thing too, because it often happens. I do mind polluting the air of Vermont and New Hampshire on my way in to teach a course in environmental studies. I just hadn't clearly confronted my own inconsistency until class that day. So much easier to poke fun at David Brower's.

A couple of hours later I made myself a formal promise. Before the end of term, I would have a pollution-free way of getting to class.

But what? I quickly ruled out a bicycle. Too far and too many hills, especially for a man my age. In January, which this was, also too much snow on the roads. A mule? I don't own a mule. A horse? Yes, that I could manage. My wife and I have two horses, and one of them is even part-Arab. There would be something attractively symbolic in using an Arabian horse to replace Arabian oil.

But twenty-six miles a day is a bit far to commute on horseback; the round trip would take at least three hours. Besides, Dartmouth no longer has any stabling facilities—at least, not on campus. There's a college-owned horse farm eight miles away, to which students can and do drive in their gas-guzzling cars when they want to go riding.

Don't think I'm picking on either Dartmouth or the horse farm in mentioning this; it's just standard American behavior. If you're a typical citizen, you drive to where you're going to jog, take a taxi to aerobics class, expect follow-cars to be present for the 10 km footrace. Once a whole pack of West Virginia teenagers swept past my farm on bicycles. They turned out, as I learned from one who stopped in my barnyard to fix his chain, to be the *jeunesse dorée* of the state—on a week's bike trip. West Virginia has ample hills of its own, better than Vermont's. But some deep instinct had led them to charter a plane and fly somewhere to do their biking.

What about selling my farm and moving into Hanover, so that I could walk to work, as professors used to? I don't want to move into Hanover. I like my farm. Well, how about a farm within walking distance of the college? There are none. Not this far into the automobile age. If there were one, I couldn't afford it.

Public transportation? There is some in Vermont, and there's also state-organized car-pooling. But the infrequent buses do not at all match my irregular working hours. Anyway, I'd still have to drive, ride a bicycle or whatever the considerable distance to the bus stop. Same problem with car-pooling—which actually I did for several years when I first lived on the farm. My first wife and I shared one car back then, and could barely afford that. If I took it to work, that left her stranded. Within three miles of us there were two other young Dartmouth families in the same situation—and at considerable inconvenience in coordinating our working schedules, we husbands managed a three-way car pool. (Husbands is not a chauvinist slip. In those days it *was* all husbands [plus bachelors and widowers] on the faculty.)

But now? Without the spur of poverty, and with my peculiar working hours, car-pooling seems just too hard.

What really suited me, as it suits most Americans, was to get to work traveling alone in my own car. Perhaps, I thought, I still could. Gasoline is not the only option. I have read about electric cars. They put out no fumes whatsoever. What if I got one of them? Then I could look Alison in the eye. At that moment my small odyssey began to prepare itself.

Remember that this was the first month of the new decade: January 1990. Electric cars are hardly common now; they were even scarcer then. I had absolutely no idea where to find one.

If you want a gas car, the whole world conspires to help you get one. There are constant ads on TV and in the magazines. There are dealers in every town, special lots where you can buy secondhand machines at low prices, whole companies devoted to auto loans, classified ads in every newspaper. It would be a rare American who couldn't name ten makes of gasoline automobiles more quickly and confidently than he or she could cite the Ten Commandments or the ten articles of the Bill of Rights. If you doubt me, try.

But I didn't know of any manufacturer of electric cars.

In January 1990 there were actually two in the United States and two abroad; I just hadn't heard of them. No great wonder: The two in the U.S. were tiny, and the two abroad didn't (and don't) sell here. I had never seen an ad for an electric vehicle, never examined one, never even passed one on the road. All I had was the bare knowledge that such things existed. It is not surprising that quite soon I extended my vow. I would give myself to the end of the year to have a pollution-free way of getting to Hanover. Because clearly I had some hunting to do.

There was a second reason I gave myself an extension (a thing I have so often, so freely, and so unwisely given to students for their papers). While I was still trying to think where and how to start looking for an electric car, another idea came rather unwelcomely into my head. The car wasn't going to be enough. Not to stop my trail of commuter's pollution. You obviously need electricity to run an electric car, and where was I going to get *that*? From the 20-amp circuit in my garage? If so, wouldn't I just be transferring the pollution from the tailpipe of my Toyota pickup to the smokestack of some power plant? Mightn't that actually make things worse than before? The Toyota at least pollutes at ground level, but power plants usually have stacks several hundred feet high, thus giving their various emissions a boost into the upper atmosphere, and helping to spread the stuff around quickly. Before I could even start the car hunt, I needed to check out power sources.

What I found was quite reassuring. There are several different ways of getting power for an electric car that either reduce pollution almost to zero or at least cut it enough to make a huge difference. Two of these ways were available to me in rural Vermont. With my goal of getting to class in as nearly pollution-free a way as possible, I naturally opted for the cleaner—and more expensive—of these methods, which was to make my own electricity with solar panels on the barn roof. (What's the other method? You'll hear later.)

That took a long time to arrange, and as it turned out, I failed to get either the electric car or the clean power source during the year 1990. I now have both, though, and I drive in to Hanover almost as guiltlessly as those earlier generations of professors walked from their houses on the edge of campus.

This book tells two stories. The first is of my own electric car: the long search to find it, the trip to bring it home from California, and finally the car's happy life as a commuter vehicle in Vermont and New Hampshire. Tied in comes the substory of finding and installing the solar panels that power the eighteen batteries in my car.

Second, the book tells some of the history of electric cars in America. I had no idea, back when I vowed to get one, that they once were so prominent. Maybe you (dear reader) also didn't know that on the first day of the twentieth century, nearly half the cars in the United States were electric. Nearly half of a very small number, I admit: On January 1, 1900, there were only a few thousand cars in the United States. But in 1910, when the number had risen to 458,-000, nearly half were still electric.

Decline was imminent, however: Gasoline cars had long since gotten both faster and capable of traveling much farther without refueling. Electrics continued to sell so well chiefly because they were so much cleaner (it was just *normal* to have greasy hands if you drove an early gasoline car) and because they were so utterly reliable about starting. Gasoline cars were not. You cranked, and then you might have to crank again, and maybe then again. You might even need a push. With an electric, you turned a key and off you went.

But when gasoline cars borrowed a trick from the enemy—that is, when electric starters were introduced in 1912—then the fight was over. Electric cars certainly didn't vanish. Numerous companies continued to make them well into the 1920s, and Detroit Electric went on until 1940. But they were no longer serious competition.

Sometime around 1970 they began to look competitive again. Not in either speed or range, which had hardly gained at all since the twenties, but in their ability to do without gas or oil (my car uses none of either), and in their ability to reduce pollution. Though I certainly didn't notice any of them at the time, several companies went into fairly large operation. In May 1974 a company called Sebring began to manufacture a little electric it called the CitiCar, and in the next two years made about 2,200 of them. At the beginning of the eighties, Jet Industries of Texas made several thousand much larger and faster Electricas. In the one year of 1985, Sir Clive Sinclair manufactured around 14,000 electric minicars in England.

These companies are all defunct, but others have replaced them. Right now, I know of four American companies that are making and selling electric cars. All are tiny, much smaller than Jet or Sir Clive's Sinclair Vehicles Ltd. My own car is the fifty-sixth made by the company I bought it from; none of the four companies is even close to the thousand mark.

But all that is about to change. Almost every major automobile manufacturer has experimental or prototype electric cars on hand, and several are already committed to mass production. General Motors is, and so is Ford. I have met people in the electric car division of both. Abroad, there are so many it's hard to keep track. Peugeot is selling electric vans not only in France but in Hong Kong. Fiat is a major producer. Nissan hopes to enter the California market in two years. BMW has a new electric car (prototype only) with one giant battery instead of fifteen or twenty standard ones, and claims it will cruise at 75 mph. The resurrection of the electric car is just beginning.

So. In the past three years I have picked up a lot of new knowledge, plus a new vehicle, and a new way of driving. (You learn that, with an electric car.) And who is responsible? First Alison, and then that entire Environmental Studies 1 class. I told them of my plans. They have not failed, even after the course ended, to keep me firmly under pressure. This book is one result.

CHAPTER 1

Finding the Car

All the electric runabouts I ever saw, while they were
very nice cars, didn't seem to go very fast or very far.
—Mr. Swift, speaking to his son in *Tom Swift and
His Electric Runabout,* 1910

O N MAY 2, 1991, I drove silently onto the freeway in Santa
Rosa, California. I was starting across the United States with
my new electric car.

I had no worries about keeping up with traffic. Unlike the early
runabouts condescended to by Mr. Swift, this car could zip along. I
was worried about distance. My farm in Vermont lay somewhat over
3,100 miles to the east. To hope to drive all that way, over the Sierras,
over the Rockies, through 1,000 miles of the Midwest, relying just on
a rack of batteries and some very small solar panels on the roof of the
car might be sheer folly.

And what if I had car trouble? There would be no handy service
stations to pull into. Ten thousand skilled mechanics for gasoline
and diesel cars practiced their craft along my route, but not one
electric car mechanic. None that worked in a garage and were reach-
able by me, anyway. I knew there were a handful of electric car
enthusiasts in Salt Lake City and another handful in Denver, but I
had no names or addresses. If the car broke down, my chief recourse
would be to call the factory back in Santa Rosa. Provided my crude
layman's account on the phone enabled them to identify the prob-

15

lem, they could tell me what repairs were needed. I might then be able to make them. I might not, too.

All this made the trip rather chancy. Certainly it seemed so to the only man with long experience in the electric car field I had ever met. This was a man who used to work for the U.S. Department of Energy, back in the days when the government supported alternative modes of transportation. "I'm in a generous mood," he had said to me a month ago. "I'll give you a one in ten thousand chance of making it."

Whether I could reach Vermont was a rather remote worry at the moment, however. Right now my concern was getting out of Santa Rosa. Electrics, as anyone who has read the Prologue knows, handle somewhat differently than gasoline cars, and my whole previous experience at the wheel of one came to less than five minutes. Going up the entrance ramp, I felt distinctly tense. Well, too late to back out now. Merging into the right lane, I put the speed up to a steady fifty-five and rolled along toward Petaluma.

Today was the culmination of a very long search. Back when I decided to buy an electric car, I knew I was going to have difficulty finding one, but I hadn't dreamt how much. So I couldn't call a dealer, drop by a used electric car lot, or anything like that. No problem (I thought). Since I work at a college, I imagined I could just use contacts. One of the delights of a good faculty is that it contains people in dozens of fields. You can nearly always find someone to tell you almost anything you need to know. I wanted to know where to buy an electric car? Fine, I'll call the Thayer School of Engineering. It's part of the college, and I know people on its faculty. Better yet, they make electric cars at Thayer. Not very many, and not to sell. Just one a year, to be precise. An entirely solar-powered, completely experimental car, built by Thayer students to be Dartmouth's entry in the annual Tour de Sol electric car race. It's the kind of all-plastic vehicle that you drive lying on your stomach, and keep running with the aid of five student mechanics. Not at all what I had in mind for my commuter car. But people who build electric vehicles must surely know who else does. The students may not, but the faculty who advise them will.

I knew two Thayer professors, and I called them both. Where, I asked, can I buy a regular battery-powered electric car that you drive sitting up and could commute to work in?

Both of them more or less patted me on the head and said, "Be patient." One of them predicted I'd have to wait about three years to get an electric commuter car. The other said five. "If you'd asked me a few years ago," this one added, "I'd have sent you to Jet Industries. I know of nothing now."

If I'd been an engineer myself, or even clever with my hands, their answers might have been different. They might then have offered to give me a little help and advice while I built my own electric car. People do that. I have since met several owners of homemade electrics, and I even know of two companies that specialize in supplying the components. But I didn't back then, and it would have made no difference if I had. Though I've come late in life to teach mostly environmental studies, and dare to call myself an environmentalist, my formal training was in literature. Such technical skill as I have lies in analyzing poems, not circuits. Oxymorons I understand just fine; rheostats confuse me. Any electric car I own needs to come from a factory.

One does not exhaust the resources of a college by asking questions of the faculty. There is also the library. Dartmouth has a huge one—a couple of million books and 20,000 journals. I waded right in. What did I find? Any amount of information about electric cars of the past (some of which will appear later in this book). Many technical articles and books about electric vehicle design at present. It was while reading these that I became familiar with the term "EV," used to cover all kinds of electric vehicles: trucks, cars, motorcycles, even golf carts.

I also found plenty of prophecy about the future. Many people had visions about the role of EVs in the year 2010 or in 2020. A somewhat smaller number took a look at a nearer future, the late 1990s, when California will be requiring a certain percentage of zero-pollution cars. That principally means electrics. From there they segued into the car that GM was planning for that market. It already existed in prototype—it's called the Impact—and I read four or five different articles about it. It sounded like a lovely car, a desirable car. I phoned GM; I also wrote them. As a result I got several handsome brochures about the Impact. None of them even hinted at an actual production date.

All that was in our library. But I found zero information on anything so small and practical as where to go to buy an electric car now. Only once did my hopes rise. That was in the spring of 1990, while I was doing a computer search of automotive journals.

A title turned up from the magazine *Road and Track,* which seemed to promise an article on the road-testing of six different Italian electric cars. Six! This at a time when I would have been sloppily grateful to hear of just one current manufacturer of electrics.

I probably should have realized at once that the article was a hoax, but my will to believe was strong. After all, I had just spent several months learning that Europe was well ahead of the United States in producing electric vehicles. I knew that at that minute there were tens of thousands of electric milk trucks cruising around Britain—small vehicles and slow, to be sure, but still genuine electrics. I had heard vague rumors (through a Swiss-born teacher in the Russian department) of a fast electric car being made in Switzerland. An engineer in Los Angeles, the friend of a friend, told me of one being developed in Sweden, though he had no address I could write to. Peugeot in France was said to have plans, too.

So why not Italy? Six makes did seem a little lavish—but then, Italy has few or no oil wells and a distinguished record of electrical innovation. Who are volts named for? Who but Count Alessandro Volta. Galvanizing? Comes from Luigi Galvani. Marconi didn't get the radio named for him, but it was a near thing. Look in older dictionaries, and you'll find the verb "to marconi," meaning to send a marconigram, or radio message. So many electric cars? It was possible.

But when I rushed down to the engineering library to look at that issue of *Road and Track,* I came on what passes with its editors for a humor piece. The article was actually about an Italian company that makes electric Dodg'em cars for amusement parks, and paints them in six colors. *Road and Track* mock-tested one of each color, solemnly reporting turning radiuses of just a foot or two, top speeds of three or four miles an hour, and so on. Very funny.

Forget the library. My next step should have been to call one of the several electric automobile clubs that exist in this country. It never occurred to me. Back then I had no idea there were such clubs.

In the end, I ran a want ad. Since I probably couldn't have afforded the kind of attention-getting, two-column, nationally published advertisement that the situation called for, I resorted to a subterfuge. In December 1990 I wrote a humorous, or would-be humorous, lament about my complete failure to find an electric car, and I kept it to the length (1,000 words) that newspapers normally allow on their Sunday op-ed pages. Actually, most of them would rather have 650 words, but they will allow a little extra. Then I sent it to the *Washington Post*. I picked this paper for two reasons. First, it had occasionally printed pieces of mine in the past. Second, it belongs to quite a large syndicate. If they took the piece, with any luck it would run in several dozen Sunday papers. They took it.

There is no doubt that advertising works. Within a week I had been offered three different used electric cars, including a Jet in Maryland and a CitiCar in New Jersey. The next week brought in several more offers of used electrics—and then something more exciting still.

I got a phone call from a man named Dick Frost, in Santa Rosa, California. "Mr. Perrin?" he said. "I understand you're looking for an electric commuter car. Well, we make them."

"We" turned out to be a firm called Solar Electric Engineering. They were a small but established company—had been selling solar-powered garden lights for a decade, did solar hot-water systems, home power plants, and so on. Now they had started to manufacture electric cars. Or, more accurately, had started to convert gasoline cars to electrics. As far as I could tell from a couple of newspaper articles that Dick mailed me—one from the *Petaluma Argus-Courier,* one from the *Santa Rosa Press-Democrat*—the company had been converting cars for a bit over a year, and had so far produced about forty. (I could have asked Dick this directly, but somehow it seemed an awfully personal question.)

So now, in January 1991 I had eight choices open to me. I could buy any of seven used EVs, or I could buy a new one from Solar Electric. Five of the used ones I ruled out at once. The 1977 CitiCar, for example, was a terrific bargain, just $2,200, but too slow for my purposes. Top speed: 38 mph. A splendid old Bradley was too expensive: $20,000. One of the Jets was offered as is—and "as is" in this case meant in need of a great many repairs, none of which I felt competent to do.

But the other two, both Jets, sounded good. If Solar Electric hadn't existed, I would certainly have bought one. Solar Electric did exist, however, and . . . I am a good enough American to have a built-in preference for new things. A sparkling new electric car sounded irresistible. I began negotiations at once.

It is somewhat unnerving to shop for a car at a distance of 3,000 miles. There is no question of test-driving, or even of finding out if the car feels right. All I had to go on were the two clippings, the information Solar Electric included in the very small brochure they sent me, and what Dick Frost told me during our increasingly frequent phone calls.

The basic facts were simple enough. Solar Electric was prepared to sell me a car for $15,700. This car, according to the brochure, would go sixty to sixty-five miles an hour, and it had a range of forty-five to sixty miles. Then you would need to stop and recharge. This you could do anywhere there was 110-volt current. In other words, you could plug into any household outlet (except the special ones for electric stoves and dryers), and most nonhousehold outlets as well.

Natural optimist that I am, I registered only the upper figures, and thenceforth thought of the car as having a cruising speed of sixty-five miles an hour and a driving range of sixty miles. Both would be more than adequate for getting me in to class.

What did this car look like? That depended on what kind of gas car got converted. Dick Frost said they liked to do Fords; the brochure mentioned Hondas as well. It would look much like any other Ford or Honda, I gathered, unless you happened to notice there was no tailpipe, or unless you lifted the hood. It would sound, of course, quite different—almost noiseless.

How expensive to run would it be? Here the brochure made strong claims for economy. According to the brochure, it took just three cents' worth of electricity to drive one of these cars a mile.

(Later, back in Vermont, testing the car, I would find that it took even less than that on level roads.)

By contrast, said the brochure, a standard car consumes about eight cents' worth of gas a mile. Well, maybe a few cars do. Most certainly do not. My Toyota four-wheel-drive, which I had already conceded in class to be a guzzler, gets just about twenty miles to the gallon. Gas at our village store fluctuates between $1.19 and $1.29 a gallon. Thus that little truck currently burns six cents' worth of gas a mile, not eight. But the electric car does better. More than twice as well.

Pitted against a car getting forty miles to the gallon, however, it would not be cheaper at all. It would actually be more expensive than the small but growing number of gasoline cars that get fifty miles to the gallon. Or perhaps it would, anyway. The tricky matter of city driving comes in here. Gasoline cars all do very much worse in city traffic than on the open road, and that's because in town they spend so much time burning gas at lights and stop signs—polluting the air and going nowhere. But an electric uses no electricity at all when it is stopped for a light, or at least the engine uses none. I guess you could have the radio on, or be running the wipers. The city mileage of an electric, Dick said one day, should be equal to or better than what it gets in the country. Maybe a fifty-miles-to-the-gallon gas car wouldn't be so much ahead.

While I was reading these agreeable statistics in the brochure and discussing them with Dick, I was also questioning him about something much less agreeable. My new car wouldn't be entirely new. I understood the reasons well enough. If Solar Electric bought new Fords and Hondas, not only would they have shiny new combustion engines to strip out and get rid of, they would wind up with prices high enough to scare off most buyers, me included. Instead of $15,700, they would be asking closer to $25,000. Why, I could have the noble Bradley for less than that.

I also understood that in many ways the car *would* be new. New engine, new batteries—sixteen or eighteen of them—new controller. New charger, new tires (special low-friction ones). In my case, new paint job. New instruments on the instrument panel. It would be enough to give me the new-car high I wished to have. And since all the specifically EV stuff would be new, enough to give me a kind of assurance I wouldn't have had with any of the seven used electrics, where something might soon go wrong and be beyond my capacity or even that of Thayer students to fix.

But I still wanted to know something about the older car that would be lurking inside my new one. Here is what I found. Solar Electric, said Dick, sent a buyer to used-car auctions. He looked for sound-bodied cars five or six years old. A bad engine was an actual asset, since it kept the price down. When they got the car back to their shop, they took out not only the motor but the entire exhaust system (an electric car needs no muffler, catalytic converter, etc.), the radiator (needs no antifreeze, either—nothing to freeze in an electric motor), and a good bit more. Then they set to work converting.

"One thing that might interest you, Noel," Dick added, "is that we don't use any salt on the roads out here." It interested me greatly. We do use salt in Vermont, and it is what ages our cars so fast. Get a car that has never tasted salt, and it matters much less whether it is brand-new or six years old.

By now it was the middle of February, and I was almost ready to order. Dick and I had discussed solar panels, and I had decided to get all the car would take. To increase that number, they would look for a little Ford Escort station wagon, and convert that. On the top they would mount four full-size solar panels. They'd put two more, smaller ones, on the hood. Solar panels are extremely expensive, and these six, installed, would add $1,800 to the car's cost.

But I was glad to pay the price. I had a new plan which I hadn't mentioned to Dick yet, or to anyone else. If this car had to come all the way from California, why have it shipped at great expense? Why not go out and get it? And drive it home under its own power. Just on batteries, the car was supposed to have a sixty-mile range, but with that big array of solar panels it should be able to go sixty-five miles or even a little more. Let's see. The car takes eight hours to charge fully. There'll be nothing to stop me from getting up and driving early in the morning, spending the day somewhere while it recharges, and driving again in the late afternoon. Maybe I can't or won't want to do that every day, but many. There will also be cloudy days, with no solar charging. So be cautious. Figure on an average of sixty-three or sixty-four miles a day, and some days double that. I'll get home in somewhere between a month and six weeks.

This idea of driving the car across the United States had an extra appeal to me because of something I had learned, reading in the college library about the early history of motorcars. The first car to cross the United States went from San Francisco to New York in the summer of 1903. It was a heroic trip. There were as yet no paved roads outside of cities, and in many parts of the West there were not even bridges over the smaller rivers. You forded. The two men who drove that first car developed a technique of gunning the car into a river, and floating across by a combination of momentum and the propeller effect they were convinced they got by keeping the rear wheels spinning. They had a wonderful and appalling time. And they were from Vermont.

So far as I knew, no electric car had crossed the country yet. Certainly none did in those early days. Couldn't have. There was no electricity in about seven-eighths of the United States. How does that square with almost half of the cars being electric? Just fine. City people owned those electrics. In 1903, city people owned nearly all the cars of any kind.

I'll give just one example. In that year there were seven Guggenheim brothers living in New York City. They were all rich. One of them had stayed faithful to horses, but the other six had converted to cars. In the spring of 1903 these six brothers decided to build a sort of family garage on West Seventy-seventh Street. Not that such buildings were called garages yet; they were called automobile stables. The Guggenheim automobile stable was a fine big one. It housed fifteen cars, eight chauffeurs, an electrician, and a full-time car washer (who probably himself was a recently converted horse groom). Of the fifteen cars, nine were electrics and six were gas.

Where there was electricity, the early EVs got around nicely. For example, that same year a man named Frank Babcock drove an electric car the 225 miles from Boston to New York. He had to stop and get charged just five times en route. In 1904 a New Yorker named Dumont took his family for a 300-mile electric car trip through New Jersey and Pennsylvania.

But then or later, no electric car that I was aware of crossed the country, and the idea that the first one might come from Vermont I found appealing. I've always liked patterns. I even liked it that Dr. Nelson Jackson of Burlington, Vermont, and Sewall Crocker, his chauffeur, had left in May 1903, and if I went out as soon as I had taught my last class, I could leave in May 1991.

Right now, however, it was February, and I hadn't even ordered a car yet. I was dithering. Mail and phone calls were still trickling in as a result of the want ad, and I kept thinking what a big country this is. Who knows what I still haven't heard about? Maybe tomorrow an even better offer will come. Dick Frost meanwhile kept pointing out that if I wanted a Solar Electric car in May, I'd better order, and send in the 25 percent deposit the company asks for. "Noel," he said, "we've got a two-month backlog of orders, and it takes three to four weeks to convert a car. We'll do whatever you want, but if you're talking about May . . ."

Two things happened in the next two days that decided me. One was that on each of those days I got a letter in response to the article. The two writers, both Californians, had the same message for me. There's this company in Santa Rosa. . . .

The prosaic explanation for these letters, I think, was that after long delay the article had just appeared in the *San Francisco Chronicle*. What it felt like was fate.

The second thing was a simple suggestion from my wife. I had been complaining to her how hard it was to shell out $17,500 for something I'd never seen. She said, "Why not talk to someone who has? Ask Solar Electric for a reference, dummy." That's a term of affection with us.

So I did. Soon I was talking to a doctor in Northern California. He had owned his converted Honda for six months.

"If you had it to do over, would you still get it?" I asked.

"Sure. I'd probably ask them to add a couple of batteries, though. I've just got sixteen, and I wish I had a little better range."

What about speed?

"I've had this car up to seventy-four." Wow!

Were the batteries a bother to take care of? No. Had he had any repairs yet? No. Anything he'd like to change besides the number of batteries? Yes. He wished the car had a more powerful heater. The tiny electric one it came with did not keep him warm.

That settled it. Who needs a fancy heater? I once had a really old truck, a '37 Dodge, with no functioning heater at all, and I got through several Vermont winters with it. All it takes is a pair of heavy gloves with wool liners (fluffy plastic won't do), and the sense not to drive on the rare days when there's a spell of freezing rain. If a dinky heater was the worst problem, I was ready to order.

The next day I sent a check for $4,375 off to Santa Rosa. I also called Dick. "Do you want us to see about shipping the car?" he asked.

"No. I think I'm going to drive it home."

"Noel, this is a car with a range of forty-five to sixty miles," he said in his deep voice.

"I know that. I'm working out a route where I can stop that often."

I was, too. I had all sorts of maps on order. For the first time in my life, I joined the AAA, precisely in order to get one of the special route maps called Triptiks that they custom-prepare for members. I think the AAA is shortsighted in some ways—they still take the position that the only proper use of gasoline taxes is to build more roads—but they are justly famous for their maps. I also followed up on a suggestion given me by a Dartmouth student named Tracy Zafian. During one of her high school summers, Tracy bicycled across the United States. She told me about the TransAmerica Bicycle Trail, which sounded marvelous. You can get these really detailed maps, she said—four miles to the inch. They're very expensive, and they're worth it.

I instantly ordered a set. Bicyclists, to be sure, aren't necessarily thinking about available electricity, but they are thinking in units of distance that seemed ideal for me.

Even though the car was now on order, I continued to have frequent conversations with Dick. He continued to voice his worry that I was planning too ambitiously; I continued to pooh-pooh his worry. "I've got May and June clear," I told him; "I'll just take as long as it needs." During one call he suggested that the engineers at Solar Electric could make a tiny flatbed trailer on which they would mount a gasoline-powered generator. I could tow this behind the car, making electricity as I went. "No way," I said. "If I were going to do that, I might as well get a gasoline car to begin with."

Thanks to the *Washington Post* syndicate, I continued to get occasional phone calls and letters from people interested in EVs. In a talky mood one evening, I boasted to one of them that if I made it, I'd probably be the first person to drive an electric car from coast to coast.

"I'm sorry to tell you that you're twenty-three years too late," he said. And then he told me about the Caltech-MIT race in 1968. One electric car set out from MIT for Pasadena, and one from Caltech headed for Cambridge, Massachusetts. First to arrive won. Both arrived.

When I looked all this up in Baker Library (the information had been there all the time, and I missed it), I found that the two cars were not entirely unaided. The Caltech entry, for example, was accompanied by six other vehicles, one of which towed a generator like the one Dick had proposed for me, only much bigger. I don't know how many escort vehicles the MIT car had; I do know that it had an eventful trip. The expensive nickel-cadmium batteries overheated, and had to be packed in ice, like lettuce in a good grocery store. The MIT car caught fire in Indiana, but not seriously. At Victorville, California, it couldn't find suitable charging facilities, and had to be towed to Pasadena. For that reason, Caltech won. Both these cars, of course, were experimental and high-tech. The traditional lead-acid batteries in my car were unlikely to need ice packs, nor was there much danger that the whole car would burst into flames. I was in a different and safer category. Safer than in a gasoline car, probably.

It would have been fun to be the first, but maybe I could still be the first to go alone. I continued to spurn the idea of a generator.

It got to be late April, and I was ready to leave. Reports from Santa Rosa said the car was nearly finished. I had my ticket to San Francisco. (Airlines are weird. I bought a round-trip ticket, not because I had any notion of using the return, but because it was cheaper than a one-way ticket.) I had dismissed the idea of taking the TransAmerica Bicycle Trail—there were actually two—because one version started out by going way north to Washington State and the other by going south almost to Mexico. I wanted to try the more direct route followed by Nelson Jackson and Sewall Crocker and several other parties in 1903—that is, heading straight for Sacramento, then on through Nevada, Salt Lake City, and Denver. I had managed to wangle a set of new Vermont plates out of the state Department of Motor Vehicles, and planned to take them out with me in my suitcase. That way I could avoid registering the car in California, and could also visibly be following in the tire tracks of Dr. Jackson. Not that he had Vermont plates on his Winton in 1903. Such things didn't exist yet.

When I say "wangle," I don't mean they were a present or something. On the contrary, they cost a good deal extra. You can register a gasoline or diesel car in Vermont for $42 a year. Buy any other kind, and the fee jumps to $73.50. I don't think this is because the state wants to encourage pollution. I think it's because they're worried about lost gasoline taxes. If the Department of Motor Vehicles hadn't been doing me a favor by issuing plates for a car that wasn't even here yet, I might have grumped a little. As it was, I thanked Sharon Smith of the DMV profusely, and made a private resolution to raise the matter of fees later, when I was home again.

On the afternoon of April 30, I went directly from the last class (for me) of the year to the Lebanon, New Hampshire, airport, and set out to get my car. I never even considered taking a mule.

CHAPTER 2

In Santa Rosa

A driver of a Ford car came up to a filling station and
asked for a pint of gasoline.
"You'd better get more," said the attendant.
"No," replied the Ford owner, "I'm weaning it."
— Ford joke, ca. 1920, quoted by RUDOLPH ANDERSON
in *The Story of the American Automobile*

A LITTLE BEFORE MIDNIGHT on Tuesday, April 30, I arrived in
San Francisco. Dick Frost and his wife were there to meet me
and drive me the fifty miles to Santa Rosa. It's not every car
salesman who would do that. But then, it's not every car salesman
who's an Annapolis graduate, or who has worked several decades as
an oil company executive.

"We're getting pretty excited about your trip," Dick said, pulling
onto an enormous freeway. "In fact, Gary has arranged a little send-
off." Gary was Gary Starr, founder and president of Solar Electric.

"What kind?"

"Oh, the local TV station and a few reporters. We've set it up for
day after tomorrow, 3:00 P.M. That's about when you wanted to leave,
isn't it?"

"That's fine," I said. "That gives me all day tomorrow and half of
Thursday to get to know the car. I want to drive it as much as
possible while I'm still near the factory."

"Drive all you want to tomorrow. Thursday morning you proba-

28

bly better go easy. You want a good charge when you leave. You need a map of Santa Rosa?"

"I've got one. I brought a ton of maps with me—AAA, local, you name it."

"Good for you. So that means you've got your whole route planned out?"

"Well, not all of it. But I know I'm going straight to Sacramento, then Carson City, and then across Nevada for four or five days on U.S. 50. That's the old Lincoln Highway."

"Mm."

Dick deposited me at the Days Inn in Santa Rosa, where someone from Solar Electric had also been busy. Days would be the site of the send-off, with TV crew and reporters, and Days was giving me a free room. I did not feel compromised. If I'd been going to feel compromised, I would have felt it about the agreement I'd made with Gary Starr a week earlier. That was to let the company paint its name on both sides of my car, and on the back, too.

Well, why not? My pickup at home, the gas guzzler, had the word "Toyota" painted clear across the tailgate. Big block letters, five inches high. And they didn't even ask.

Gary not only asked, he was happy to go along with my tight eastern reticence. I was perfectly willing to have the car identified as an EV, but I didn't want it to look like a traveling billboard. No fear. The messages were to say "Solar Electric Vehicle" in letters a modest two inches high. Neat but not gaudy, as people used to say when I was young. In fact, it was more description than advertisement.

Solar Electric has an office-and-store on one of the main streets of Santa Rosa, and a tiny factory half a mile away. Next morning I walked over to the store about 9:00 o'clock. Under my arm I had tucked my two green Vermont plates. Time for a drive. I thought I'd probably go over the range of hills east of Santa Rosa, and down into the Napa Valley. It seemed to be no more than twenty miles. I love visiting wineries. Don't have the chance much, in Vermont. I was only sorry that since I needed to keep weight down, I couldn't buy five or ten cases to take with me.

Dick was out front having a cigarette. No smoking allowed in the building. He put it out, and we went into the store, which was full of eco-products: trays of rechargeable batteries, stacks of recycled paper products, rows of compact fluorescent lights. In one corner was a long, low convertible, painted white—an EV with sex appeal. Back in the office part I met Gary Starr, a man in his thirties with an inventor's intense blue eyes. Dick and I finished some paperwork. "So let's get the car," I said when that was done. I had been looking forward to this moment for a year and a quarter now.

"Noel, we're running a little behind. It's not quite ready. We can go see it, though."

Over in the factory yard we threaded our way through a group of about a dozen old mail vans waiting to be converted—and there in one bay of the building was my car. It wasn't sexy, like the white convertible, but it was beautiful. It gleamed with fresh red paint. The discreet white lettering on the sides and back had been done in a good typeface—not a bit like the clunky letters on the Toyota. Four solar panels covered the entire roof; they looked terrific. A young technician was just getting ready to mount two smaller ones on the hood. He instantly noticed the green plates under my arm. "Brought your own, did you? That's neat. I can put them on for you." He looked at them for a moment. "Where is Vermont, anyway?"

Now a slightly older man in a lab technician's coat came over—he might have been thirty, even thirty-one. Dick formally introduced me. "Noel, I want you to meet Neil Sinclair. He's our vice-president, and he's the one besides Gary who knows most about electric cars."

"Do you happen to know when mine will be ready?" I asked. My tone wasn't nasty, just hopeful.

"It's going to be tomorrow. We're doing some extra things because of your trip. You're asking an awful lot of a commuter car, and we want to give you the best possible chance of making it." There was something in *his* tone that I found very sobering.

On the way back, Dick was sober, too. "Noel, I'm not comfortable about your taking U.S. 50," he said. "Triple-A in Vermont may have put you on it, but I wish you'd talk to Triple-A here. It's real desert."

Since I wasn't going to any wineries, and since Neil and Dick's sobriety was proving highly infectious, I readily agreed. What had seemed simple enough back in Vermont, and even when I talked to the expert in Washington, was beginning to look formidable.

The AAA office in Santa Rosa is huge. There were three people staffing the map-and-tour counter alone. The one I talked to said she had never personally driven U.S. 50, but she'd heard bad things. She gave me another map of Nevada, my third.

"Let's call the Nevada state police," said Dick when we got back to his office. He did, and got Sergeant Shemick in Carson City.

"That's the loneliest highway in the United States," said Sergeant Shemick. "You can go a hundred miles without even a house. Before he takes it, he better talk to Ron Hill in Nevada DOT."

This time I made the call. Ron Hill said firmly not even to consider U.S. 50 in my electric car. He would bet money I didn't make the grade at Austin. So what did he recommend? "You take Interstate 80, or you're not going to get across Nevada."

It's amazing how easy it is to change a long-held plan once you start feeling scared. Not only did I shift my route on the spot, I changed my mind about a generator. I still had no thought of towing one on a little cart, but I decided it would be mere prudence to have one stashed in the car for emergencies. By midafternoon I owned one, had tested it, bought and filled a small gas can.

On Thursday morning I again showed up at the store. It was 9:00 A.M.

"Noel, the car's almost ready," Dick said. "You can take it out around 11:00 or 11:30."

I couldn't, though. Still a little to do. We rescheduled for 2:00 P.M. Dick took me to an auto supply store to get a little battery-test meter he thought I should have along; Gary gave me an official-looking letter to show to suspicious motel and filling station owners. It said that the most electricity my car could possibly take (at standard West Coast utility rates) was $1.50 worth. He also made me a present of two heavy-duty extension cords. They were bright orange, fifty feet long each, equipped with an adapter so that I could plug in to two-prong as well as three-prong outlets, could even draw my charge from a light bulb socket. "You'll find these handy in Nevada," he said with a grin.

After that I fooled around in bookstores and malls, and enjoyed the flowers of Santa Rosa. Just before 2:00, back at Days, I got caught by a phone interviewer from a radio station in San Francisco. When

Dick and I finally reached the shop at 2:30, the car had gone. It was over at Days Inn for the send-off. Back we hurried.

One TV crew and one reporter were there, and most of the staff of Solar Electric. Plus a number of drop-ins: passersby who saw the solar panels and the neat white lettering, and who stopped to ask questions. How far will it go? How fast will it go? Can you drive on rainy days? Yes, I can drive on rainy days. It will cruise at sixty-five, I said, with somewhat more assurance than my personal knowledge then warranted. But I did not say it had a range of sixty miles. Dick and Neil had succeeded in convincing me that this was a variable. That depends, I said. Might be as little as forty-five miles, might be as much as sixty.

Then the TV crew packed up and left, the reporter got in his car, and the staff went back to work. Around quarter to four I finally took my test drive. It consisted of running Neil the half mile back to the shop while he gave me urgent last-minute instructions. "There are two settings on the charger," he said. "Always start charging on Low. Don't ever step on the accelerator when the car's out of gear. You can wreck an electric motor that way. Be sure to water your batteries once a month."

At four o'clock I had my real send-off. The car was loaded with maps, AAA guidebooks, the generator, the orange cords, luggage for a five- or six-week trip. I did not have either the two automatic pistols or the ax that Dr. Nelson Jackson and Sewall Crocker took with them in 1903. I did have nine half-pint cans of maple syrup (my own product) for possible swapping. I'd left home with even more, but Dick Frost and his wife had gotten some, and so had Tish, the publicity manager at Days Inn. One freebie deserves another.

Neil and the technicians waved. My electric car, the fifty-sixth made by Solar Electric Engineering, pulled out of the shop and began its long journey.

CHAPTER 3

The First Day Out

Mr. Swift: About how far do you expect your car will go
with one charging of the battery?
Tom: Well, if I can make it do 300 miles I'll be satisfied.
—VICTOR APPLETON, *Tom Swift and His Electric
Runabout,* 1910

WHEN I pulled onto the freeway in Santa Rosa, I had only the vaguest idea of where I'd spend the first night. I was still heading for Sacramento—the change to I-80 made no difference there. But how far should I go? Dick Frost had suggested I stop at Petaluma—but that was only twenty miles down the valley. At twenty miles a day, it would take me nearly half a year to get home. Maybe I can't do my full sixty miles today, I thought, or even forty-five, but I'll be damned if I'll settle for twenty.

Traffic was heavy on California 101. I stayed in the right lane. My mind was busy going over all the last-minute instructions Neil Sinclair had given me. How to handle hills seemed the most important right now. An electric motor, unlike a gasoline engine, has no braking power, and unless one's EV is equipped with regenerative braking (which means you can convert your momentum back into power for the batteries), one is therefore coasting down hills. The more speed I could pick up on the way down, the farther I could get up the next rise before I had to use any electricity. I therefore stayed a good 50 yards behind the mail truck that was rolling along in front of me.

Whenever we came to a hill, I let the space increase to 100 yards. No
one honked, or cut furiously in, as they would around Boston. Instead, the stream of cars just whirled on past in the left lane, leaving
the right lane to me, the mail truck, a few other trucks, and four
teenagers in an open jeep.

About every thirty seconds I glanced at my fuel gauge. This is a
very different instrument on an electric car than on a gas car. On a
gas car, the gauge measures something substantial, even Euclidean:
the number of gallons left in your tank. It's so easy to measure that a
luxury car may well be equipped to give you continuous computer
readouts of how many more miles you can drive at your present
speed before you'll need to stop at a filling station. Even the simplest
car gives you a pretty good indication. The needle may go down
slightly faster from Half to Empty than it did from Full to Half, but it
never suddenly jumps down. On most cars, even after the needle
points to Empty, you've still got enough gas to go another fifteen or
twenty miles.

What an electric car has is a voltage gauge. And what is a volt,
besides a memorial to Count Volta? It's a unit of force, not of quantity, and a little bit comparable to the speed with which a river is
flowing, as opposed to the volume of water in it. I find it hard to
think in volts.

The fuel gauge on my car was a round black dial about two
inches in diameter. It was labeled "BATTERY CAPACITY." Just below
these words was a tiny rectangular window, marked "E" at one end
and "F" at the other. When you turned the car key on, a little green
bar appeared somewhere in that window. That much I had perceived
even in Santa Rosa. At the time I left, the bar was right where I
wanted it to be: all the way to the end marked "F."

I don't think I had driven more than two miles when a second
green bar suddenly appeared beside the first one, and then the first
one gradually faded. I didn't like to take my eyes off the road much,
despite the long space between me and the mail truck, but in repeated hasty glances I was able to work out that the new bar expressed a percentage. I was now down to 90 percent of whatever Full
meant. Even as I watched, a third green bar appeared, and the second
faded. Oh, lord. Still only seven miles from Santa Rosa, and I was

down to 80 percent. Lower, actually. One of the pieces of information I retained from the many Neil Sinclair had given me half an hour ago was that the gauge went down a great deal faster during the second half than during the first.

Another green flash as I climbed a small hill, and now the batteries were down to 70 percent. But 70 percent of what? That is hard to pin down. My car has eighteen batteries. One is a big twelve-volt marine battery, and that has its own circuit and its own special solar panel to keep it topped off. It runs the lights, the radio, the windshield wipers—and maybe in winter the heater? I'm not sure about that.

The other seventeen batteries are identical 6-volt deep-discharge batteries; they were originally designed for golf carts. In my car, they are all wired in series, which means that the voltage builds. One of these batteries alone: 6 volts. Two wired together: 12. Three: 18. And so on. Seventeen of them working together, like seventeen people pulling on a rope, have a theoretical capacity of 102 volts and an actual capacity a good deal higher. For reasons I don't fully understand, you can charge a 6-volt battery up to well over 7 volts. If my battery array were to be totally charged up, it would be carrying a voltage of somewhere around 130 volts. It clearly was not full when I left Santa Rosa, or the gauge wouldn't have dropped a bar after only two miles. Not too surprising; after all, they were working on the car all morning and into the afternoon; there was no time for a final topping off. Another green flash. Then another. There may have been one or two that I missed seeing. As best as I could tell from hasty worried glances, the gauge was now on 30 percent. I was just coming up to the Petaluma exit, and I had been seventeen miles. I'm damned if I'll stop now, but I don't want to run out of electricity, either. I pull onto the shoulder, study the gauge—it *is* on 30 percent—and then turn off the power. I get out one of my California maps. There is a little town called Ignacio about fifteen miles ahead. Seventeen I've been, fifteen to go; surely thirty-two miles isn't too much to ask of these batteries. Even if I did learn earlier today that they won't hold their absolute top charge until they've been through fifteen or twenty cycles of being filled and then drawn down.

I am much encouraged when I turn the key back on, because the green bar has jumped back up to 40 percent. I had read about this happy phenomenon in accounts of the old turn-of-the-century electrics. If you run out of juice, just pull over to the side of the road and wait ten minutes. The batteries will partially repolarize, and you can drive a few miles more. Now I know from experience that it's true. Some of the lead sulfate goes back to being pure lead, some of the sulfuric acid is restored; you get a small gift of power. Try that when you run out of gas. Just pull over and see if a couple of quarts condense in your tank. Good luck.

Beyond Petaluma I move into farm country. Dairying, looks like. I see plenty of Holstein cattle, no motels. Sure to be one in Ignacio, though.

But I'm not to Ignacio yet—nowhere near. The green bar had flashed back down to 30 percent less than three miles past Petaluma, and a few miles later it vanished altogether. Now there is a yellow bar on the gauge. I do not at all want to begin this trip by being stranded on a freeway. I slow down to forty-five, and begin to look anxiously for an exit. None in sight. I wish my wife were here with the farm truck—I may need a tow. But two miles later I come to an exit marked "Business 101." Even though I see absolutely no business around the exit, just bare hills and one green pasture, I get off the freeway.

Now what? Shall I go north or south on Business 101? It looks equally unpromising either way. I pull over and get out. To the south, which is the direction I'm headed (I'll get to turn east very shortly), Business 101 rises to the top of a low hill. Maybe I'll walk up it, and see if I can spot any businesses in the next valley, or at least a house with electricity. But then a laundry truck comes along. I wave my arms violently, and the driver stops.

"Are you from around here?" I ask. He is. "You don't happen to know if there's a motel anywhere near?"

"Hell, yes. Go on over the hill. You'll find it on the right, not much over a mile."

About three minutes later I pull into a Travelodge. It is 5:00 P.M. I am one hour into my journey home, and I have gone twenty-seven miles.

The desk clerk is a young woman of college age with long dark hair and a great fondness for the word "okay." I ask for a room. "We're just about full, okay. All I've got is one king-size room, okay, on the third floor, and that would be seventy-two dollars, okay."

It's not particularly okay, particularly coming right after two free nights at Days Inn. I wish my mileage and her room price could be switched. And being on the third floor is going to make plugging in a bit tricky.

But I don't dare drive even another mile on yellow. (Later, as I know the car better, I will get bolder. I will even know that there are two yellow bars, not just one.) I pass over my credit card. When she has run it through her little machine, I tell her about the electric car, and produce the letter from Solar Electric. She is not much interested. "Okay, I'll tell the manager after he finishes his nap. Here's your key, okay."

By good fortune, 318 with its two king-size beds is a corner room at the far end of the building. I can squeeze my car almost directly below it, between the laundry room and the tiny swimming pool. I take one of the fifty-foot orange cords up with me, plug in to a wall socket, and then, Rapunzel-style, lower the free end out the window. I run down again and connect the car, remembering to set the charger on Low. It begins to hum very softly and to recharge at the rate of fourteen amperes. Neither an elderly Chinese man having a cigarette near the pool nor two Mexican-looking cleaning people pay the faintest attention. Presently I walk half a mile down Business 101 to the very small town of Novato and have dinner at an intensely local Italian restaurant called Capra's. Tomorrow I will do better.

CHAPTER 4

The Second Day

Any owner of an up-to-date car . . . may confidently
expect to keep to a 100 mile a day schedule.
—Editorial in *The Horseless Age,* August 17, 1904

I WAS so eager to do better that the next morning I woke at 4:00. It
was still completely dark outside. I'd have liked to jump in the
car and get moving toward Nevada, but another prudent thought
restrained me. The car would be good for just about an hour's driving; then it would need a new charge. Where exactly did I propose to
get this at 5:00 A.M.? Certainly there would be all-night restaurants
and twenty-four-hour filling stations in the towns along my route.
But I didn't know their locations. I didn't even know which town I'd
be hunting in. A frantic search on yellow bar did not appeal.

So I studied my maps some more, and then dozed a little. I
showered and shaved and did some repacking. Finally, around 6:30 I
unplugged the car and got in. The green bar was on Full, and it
looked as if the charge was going to be a present from Travelodge.
Either that or the manager had not yet finished his nap.

Actually, about half the charge I could be said to have earned.
Room 318, being king-size, had a king-size air conditioner also. One
that big consumes about 1,100 watts, and during an overnight stay
in hot weather a guest could easily use twelve kilowatt-hours or

more. But I had never turned it on. I *had* plugged my car in, and the maximum number of kilowatt-hours I could have fed into it was about seventeen. Make that two-thirds.

I drove silently down Business 101, which was just beginning to wake up, and then turned east on the three-lane road that skirts San Pablo Bay. Wisps of fog were drifting across it, and obviously this is a common occurrence. For ten miles there were polite, insistent signs: PLEASE USE YOUR HEADLIGHTS. I as politely ignored them. The mist was light, my bright red car showed up clearly, and I stayed in the right lane. I didn't see that I was making myself a traffic hazard. And I was determined to make good mileage today: driving until the car ran low on electricity, recharging, driving again. Even though my rational mind said that having the headlights on shouldn't shorten the driving range one inch—that power comes from a different battery—it still felt better to leave them off.

For the first segment my modest goal was Vallejo, twenty-two miles from the Travelodge. Vallejo was where I would commit myself to the great traffic river: Interstate 80. Breakfast for me, juice for the car before I get on *that,* I thought. Only prudent.

But the green bar still showed 50 percent as I inched through heavy construction coming into Vallejo, and then reached the entrance to I-80. Though my stomach was now on E, I swung boldly on. There was soon a low hill, then another, then a third. Going up one of these, I passed my first vehicle ever: a giant diesel truck leaving a plume of dark smoke. I felt light and clean, skimming by it. I was hardly back in the right lane when I skimmed past a big sign that announced the next town would be Fairfield, population 80,-000.

If you live, as I do, in a village of 300, a place the size of Fairfield feels big. A person could get lost. A person could decide to stay the hell out. I was still alternately making and rejecting that decision, when just before Fairfield I saw something that suited my needs exactly. There was an exit. A great cluster of gas stations and fast-fooderies grouped themselves around it. Farmland showed in the background.

I gratefully pulled off. The gauge was still on green bar; I could have gone further. But I'd done thirty-three miles, and it was definitely time for breakfast.

The first gas station I came to sold Chevron. Chevron, the very company Dick Frost had worked for, whose gas he had helped to bring to Tahiti. I pulled in. The owner, a jokey man, took a look at my car and fleetingly grinned.

"What's up? You want your solar panels tuned?"

"The panels are fine. I need to get a battery charge."

"Sure. We can do that. It'll cost you seven fifty."

I grumbled a little, pointing out that the car, which wasn't fully discharged, would be taking about a dollar's worth of current. But I was too hungry to argue really well. I left the car charging on high (deliberately), and walked across I-80 on the side of a rather scary two-lane bridge. I was heading for Jason's, the restaurant in a truck stop on the westbound side of I-80. The young mechanic who helped me plug in at the Chevron station had told me it had the best food at the exit.

At Fairfield, the Great Traffic River is nearly as wide as the Mississippi. Many lanes each way. It is difficult, crossing over it on foot, with hundreds of huge trucks pounding along below, to avoid reflecting how quickly you would cease being even a spot on the pavement, were you to fall. I would have liked a sidewalk and maybe even a nice balustrade to hold on to. But this bridge had not been designed for walkers.

Jason's was as much better than the fast-fooderies as the junior mechanic at Chevron had promised. It was also a revelation of the amenities of trucker life.

What I saw when I walked into Jason's was a roomful of gabby truckers. The restaurant has a row of booths on one side, and a three-section counter on the other. Each section is U-shaped, and seats twelve people. Each comes equipped with four telephones. They sit there on the counter, casually, along with the salt and pepper—unless, of course, some burly driver in coveralls has one of them in his burly hand and is making a credit card call to his wife in Alabama.

I'd never seen anything like it. Every booth also had a phone. In the second booth, a small, elegant black driver was deep in conversation with what was obviously his teenage son. Next to the Alabaman, a man with a big order of hash browns was hotly discussing his bill of lading with some dispatcher in Chicago. Altogether, nine phone conversations were going on when I entered. I'd hardly got my orange juice when a tenth began. This one originated outside. A voice said quietly over a loudspeaker, "Jim Murphy, you have a call on Line One."

Passenger car eating places have a lot to learn from trucker eating places.

After a three-egg breakfast I crossed the fearful bridge again and took a stroll around a nascent shopping mall, which was being laid out next to a drive-in auto insurance office. I had hours to kill while the car charged.

There was not much to see where the shopping mall is planned, except some remarkably wide roads, and about 9:30 I drifted back to the Chevron station. What I found was that I'd wasted an hour and a half. I should not have started my charger on High. I had done it, of course, to speed things up. I figured a service station with power tools would have heavy-duty wiring, but in this case I was wrong. My car had popped every circuit breaker they had.

I reset the charger on Low. This time I stuck around to make sure it worked. It did just fine.

While I was there, the car got its first visitor since Santa Rosa. An old man with a rancher's wrinkled face and a big hat with a band of silver birds around it came over and started asking questions about the solar panels. He said he'd seen a solar-powered electric lawn mower advertised for sale on TV. Couldn't remember the name, alas, because it's a machine I'd love to have.

He asks if I can drive on rainy days. He asks how far I can go on a charge, and my answer reminds him of a joke he says he once played on his wife. They have a cat, a greedy one. He told his wife that the cat drank some gasoline he had poured in a dish, to use in washing oily motor parts. With a yowl, the cat tore out of the house. It ran up a tree, back down, up another tree, down again, and out into a field. Suddenly it keeled over.

"Was it dead?" asks the wife.

"No, just ran out of gas."

While the old man is still examining the car and telling me stories, the owner of the station reappears. He has a friend with him, who seems to be the owner of the 76 station a couple of hundred yards away. They are about to go out for coffee. The friend pauses to take a look at my batteries and solar panels. He tells me he likes the car. To the owner, as they get in his pickup, he says, "I guess we just seen a taste of the future."

"Don't expect *me* to like it," the owner answers. "I'm in the petroleum business."

You don't have to get a full charge every time you plug in an electric car. In fact, on a trip like this it would be foolish to try. One of the peculiarities of battery charging is that the more nearly full the batteries are, the slower the electricity goes in. It's not like filling a gas tank, where the last gallon gets pumped at exactly the same velocity as the first. Charging a set of fully discharged batteries on standard household current, the power might initially go in at the rate of 14 amps. Seven or eight hours later, when the charge is almost complete, it might be going in at only 2 amps.

Still, right now the car has been drinking its juice for only about half an hour, and that is not enough. I have more time to kill. I have already walked out Pittman Road to the drive-in auto insurance office. Now I walk out the other main road, which is called Central Place. It is dead-end. Most of the way out to the dead end you pass nothing but motels, gas stations, and fast-fooderies. Then gas stations, fast-food places, and motels. But at last comes something different. It is called Camper's World. Here is a huge fenced yard full of recreational vehicles bigger than I have ever seen before. Far bigger than the school buses at home. Most are parked; a few are moving about. Some have motorboats hitched on behind; other tow cars. The ones in motion seem to have each an aging couple up front, looking as insignificant as the pilot fish in front of a shark. I wonder how many EVs like mine it will take to balance out one giant RV like theirs. Let's see, if they get five miles to the gallon . . .

By 11:00 I am back at the Chevron station. I'm sitting in the car, looking yet again at a map of Nevada, when the charging gauge suddenly drops to zero. The station manager, a blond young guy, has unplugged me; he needs the circuit for garage work. "Just be five minutes," he says. When fifteen minutes pass, I ask him if it isn't time to reconnect. "Soon as I can," he says. "We got cars to fix." I decide to leave with my partial charge. As I go in the office to pay, I notice a price list up on the wall; one item is $5.50 for battery charging. I point this out to the manager.

"Yeah, but that's for one battery, not eighteen," he says. Not being able to think of an adequate answer, I pay my $7.50 and leave.

The car does well on its partial charge. I get another thirty-two miles, to Davis, and pull off the Great Traffic River at the university exit. The gauge is still green bar, though the lowest one.

Just off the exit there is a big convenience store with six gas pumps. I stop and go inside. "I'd like to get a fill-up for my car," I say to the late-teens boy at the cash register. "Only it's an electric car, and I need an electric fill-up."

"No problem," he says.

He looks around and finds an unused three-prong plug near the ice machine at the back of the store. Then he helps me run one of my orange cords in the door, right over the counter, and on back to the plug. He finds a couple of mats to lay over it so that customers won't trip. "Now about paying," I say. I show him Gary's letter, and say my usual policy (I just invented it) is to pay double. He readily agrees; I hand over three dollars.

Outside, a small crowd has gathered to look at the car. Two of them, young men named Paul and Mike, start telling me about a three-wheeled electric car they've seen on a TV program called "Beyond Tomorrow"—they say it went from Los Angeles to Washington, D.C., in 1990. So there have been at least three cars ahead of me.

Just then a middle-aged man in a white polo shirt and white pants gets out of a car and hurries over. "I am the owner," he says. "You can't do that here."

I instantly unplug. The teenager at the cash register quietly hands me back my three dollars. Paul and Mike go into a quick huddle, and then invite me to come with them to where I *can* plug in.

They get in Paul's car, and I follow them three miles to a small pizzeria and delicatessen. Paul guides me around back, between a couple of Dumpsters, and plugs the car in. "On the house," he says.

It turns out that Paul owns a small refrigeration business. When he stopped to look at my car, he was on his way to the pizza place to fix the compressor. Now he is simply going to deduct three dollars from the bill he gives to Moe, who owns the place.

It was about 1:00 o'clock when Paul plugged the car in. It stayed there by the Dumpsters, quietly charging, for the rest of the afternoon. Paul and Mike meanwhile fixed the compressor, and then took me on the strangest guided tour I have ever been on. The centerpiece was a flying saucer factory. I took it for granted that Paul was testing eastern gullibility when he said there was a man in Davis who built flying saucers, and he would show me one. But he did.

Paul drove us to an anonymous-looking building about forty feet by seventy, set on a couple of acres of parkland. Ignoring an office entrance at the front, he drove straight around back and into an empty parking lot. "I hate to go in front doors," he said. "There's always someone that wants to stop you."

There was no such person out back. Paul cautiously opened a large sliding door—and we found ourselves looking in at a large empty workspace. On one side a flying saucer was parked. It was round as a doughnut, made of dark blue plastic, and around the rim were eight jet engines. In the middle, the doughnut hole, there was a seat for the operator and a battery of controls. The whole thing was about ten feet in diameter.

I felt very much an intruder, looking in the back door of the flying saucer factory. So did Mike, who suggested it was time to go now. But Paul said to me, "You want to see it up close?" The workspace was empty, though clearly there were people in other parts of the building. I could hear someone on a loudspeaker calling for Carl to take Line 2. I did not at all want to be caught if Carl suddenly walked in. Neither did I want to seem timid. Paul and I walked over to the saucer, while Mike stayed by the door and served as lookout. No one saw us, and a couple of minutes later we were safely outside, and heading to our next sight.

"You do this sort of thing much?" I asked Paul.

"No guts, no glory," he answered.

"That's his favorite saying," Mike added.

A little after five I unplugged the car. Paul and Mike were there to see me off. I gave each of them one of the half-pint cans of syrup. Then I headed back toward I-80.

An hour later I had made it successfully through Sacramento at rush hour, keeping up easily with tens of thousands of gas cars. I was approaching the town of Roseville. The green bar was down to 30 percent, and it seemed a good time to stop. I took the second Roseville exit. What I found was a lot of very wide (and totally empty) streets called things like Sunrise and Eureka, but no town, and certainly no motels. It was just like last night, only this time the bar had gone through yellow and down to the red or final bar before I finally found a motel that disguised itself under the name Oxford Suites. Here I easily got a first-floor, end-of-row room. It cost sixty-one dollars, with a free drink of electricity for the car thrown in. Two minutes later I was raising the hood and showing the front batteries to a nattily dressed alternative energy expert from Oregon.

"Vermont, eh?" he said. "You must have awfully good batteries to have driven way out here. You have regenerative braking, too?"

"Don't I wish," I said.

It had been a good day, the kind of day I had planned on. On three charges, I had been 101 miles—and if they hadn't unplugged me so freely at the Chevron station, maybe I could have done 120. Vermont began to seem quite possible.

CHAPTER 5

The Sierra Nevada

That hills have no terrors for the modern electric car is
now well understood.
—FRANK W. SMITH, "The Electric's Progress,"
Collier's, January 10, 1914

I LEFT Roseville at 7:30 on the morning of May 4. My next goal was
Reno. Even though that remarkable city is just 120 miles east of
Roseville, I figured it would take me two days to get there. And
the best part of a week to get across the rest of Nevada. I had come to
the mountains.

Electric cars have never been much good at mountains, though
they are better now than they used to be. In the early days of automobiles, only steam cars went uphill with any real speed. One conse-
quence was that people who owned steamers loved to organize hill-
climbing contests, so as to embarrass and humiliate their friends
who had gasoline or electric cars. In the first years of this century
there was an annual hill-climbing event in eastern Massachusetts.
The cars had to get up a steep hill one-fifth of a mile long. Up until
1904, the record for that hill was a steamer blazing up at 42 miles an
hour. The best any gas car had done was 17 mph, and as for poor
electrics, the speediest of them came crawling up at 9 mph. But in
1904 the steamers got a shock. That year the winner was a gasoline
car. It zoomed up the hill at 48 miles an hour, closely followed by a
steamer going 45. As for electrics, they gained, too—but not enough

to impress anyone. The winning electric crawled slightly faster than any EV had the year before, and got up the hill at 10 mph.

I perhaps shouldn't say that this wouldn't impress *anyone*. Some other electric car owners—in 1904—would have been downright awed. I'm thinking, for example, of a man in Providence, Rhode Island, who commuted to work in an electric. At one point in his daily trip, he had to go up a very steep hill—12 percent grade. Up the car went, all right. But at 4 mph.

Little hills like that one in Rhode Island—or those on Business 101—certainly do hold no terrors for the modern electric. My 1991 Solar Electric had not had the faintest trouble with any slope so far.

But now I was coming up to the Sierra Nevada, the Snowy Mountains. Between me and Reno lay Donner Pass, where the unfortunate emigrants ate each other in 1846. Donner Pass is 7,200 feet higher than Roseville. My little car would have to do the equivalent of driving up the side of the Empire State Building six times. It was only because I had shifted my route to the interstate, where it's all grades designed for heavy trucks, that I expected to make the summit at all. My new owner's manual (a couple of stapled sheets) was quite explicit about climbing. "Avoid steep hills," it said. "Take a more level alternative route if possible." This, of course, *was* my alternative route.

The minute I left Roseville the road began to climb. For the first time the car felt a little sluggish. Up until now it had responded like a living thing to my lightest touch on the accelerator. If I had driven mostly between forty-five and fifty-five miles an hour so far, it was because I was extending range, not because I couldn't have gone faster.

Even now, the car started out just fine. These were only foothills it was going through, and it rolled along at a steady fifty. Put me and the car in a time machine, and we could have gone back and won that Massachusetts hill-climbing race.

But as the road kept rising mile after mile, the car began to tire. By the time I'd gone fifteen miles, it was clear I wouldn't reach Emigrant Gap, as I'd hoped, or even the minuscule town of Gold Run. I was mostly going forty now, and the gauge was dropping fast.

Twenty-two miles beyond Roseville, it dropped to the final green bar. An exit called Meadow Vista was just coming up. I saw no motels, gas stations, or fast-fooderies. In fact, no traces of human habitation at all. Just steep wooded hillsides. It struck me that it might be a good idea to pause and look at my map, and see where I might next be able to get a charge. I pulled over and got the map out. Yes, a little town called Colfax was only another four miles.

But when I turned the key back on, I got a nasty shock. The place where the last green bar had been was dark. So were the yellow bar slots. But the red bar was gleaming. It is a habit of storage batteries and of the voltage gauges that report on them to keep up a bold front while you are driving, and then to do a partial collapse when you stop. It happens regularly. Wait a little, and there's a partial recovery, as I've mentioned.

But I didn't know what would happen on this damned mountain. The recovery might take me only a mile or two, or it might get me to Colfax and beyond. I didn't know. What I knew was that the car had gone to red bar for the second time in two days, and that it was making me horribly nervous.

I didn't even consider trying to go on to Colfax. I drove the few hundred yards to the Meadow Vista exit at a cautious 30 mph, went down the ramp, pulled over on a side road, and stopped. It was a beautiful sunny green-and-gold morning. Everything was serene in Meadow Vista, except me. There were no cars on this mountain road, a narrow two-laner, the smallest road I had yet seen in California. The only action was a bit of birdsong.

In about five minutes a pickup truck came along. I was lurking by the stop sign, so I could easily ask the driver where the nearest garage or store or house was. "There's a store half a mile over that way," he said, pointing across the interstate.

Still on red (not much recovery yet), I drove to Oliver's Store. This was the old California, not the new. Except that the pumps out front were selling unleaded gas, nothing seemed to have changed since 1950. And not all that much since 1850, when every store in California was also a bar. Oliver's continues to be bar as well as grocery store, and both bar and store are in the same small room. A couple of people were sitting at the bar right now: a somewhat sultry-looking woman in black, and a plump man in a big hat. It was 8:10 A.M.

Judi, the fortyish proprietress, first said she had no place for cars to plug in, and then, perhaps appalled by the sight of a gray-haired man looking as if he might cry, recalled that there *was* an old outside plug on the wall behind the building. I brightened at once. Going out back, I found the ancient two-prong outlet under the eaves. I removed the mud nest some bird built on it long ago, and got my adapter from the glove compartment of the car. Bless Gary. A minute later Judi was tucking three dollar bills into the cash register, and the car was beginning to recharge—at 9 amps. Whether I set the charger High or Low didn't make the slightest difference; either way the batteries got 9 amps. It must be an old 10-amp circuit. This is going to take a long time.

What are my plans for when the car is finally charged up—say, at 5:00 or 6:00 P.M.? I don't know. Up until half an hour ago, of course, my plan was very clear—to keep heading east until I reach Vermont. East still seems like a good idea; it's all this *up* that has me baffled. So far the car has climbed 2,000 feet from Roseville. It must climb 5,200 feet more before it rolls across the top of Donner Pass. As I now realize, that's going to take two full charges and most of a third. Then there's the ice-cream run down to Reno. But after that? After that there's 360 miles of empty Nevada awaiting me. I don't even have to look at the map; I know the obstacles by heart. Golconda Summit, 5,154. Twin Summit, 5,672. Emigrant Pass, 6,114. Pequop Summit, 6,967. Silver Zone Pass, 5,940. After that come the mountains of Utah.

I hate to give up the idea of driving my car home across the country. I also hate the idea of what it might take to keep going.

I *could* manage the trip, probably. The gasoline-powered generator has been sitting in the back of the car, waiting for just such a moment as this. I could have used it this morning, if there had been no Oliver's. I can use it whenever needed. There will be power available some places in the mountains, such as Gold Run, California, and Golconda, Nevada. When there isn't, and I find myself on yellow bar partway up some pass, I can pull off the road, lift the generator out, and set it down a few feet behind the car. Start it up, and six to eight hours later I'm ready to go on. What if it shouldn't start? Well, I could always turn around and coast back down. A pity this car doesn't have regenerative braking, so I could be recharging as I went. My next EV will have it.

Three objections rise up at once. One is boredom. To sit by the side of I-80 for six or eight hours while the car charges up might prove kind of interesting, if done just once or twice. I probably wouldn't dare leave the car and the throbbing generator to take a mountain hike. But a certain number of good Samaritans might stop to see what was going on—and they'd be people worth meeting. I'd probably encounter a few state troopers as well—and it would be in their benign mode, not writing me a ticket in cold, correct silence, but offering friendly advice, and being curious about how the car worked.

As a daily habit, however, it would soon pall.

Second, I think it might hurt my pride to spend much time squatting on the shoulder of I-80 while an endless stream of cars and trucks roared by. It would put me in much the same position that another electric car owner found himself eighty-eight years ago. He was a doctor. Turn-of-the-century physicians bought a lot of electric cars, because electrics started much more reliably than early gas cars, and nothing is more annoying than to dash off to an emergency, only your car won't start. The doctors also liked it that you didn't get your hands oily, just as you were supposed to be delivering a baby or whatever.

Dr. M. H. Bailey was an EV pioneer, the second person in a city of 100,000 to buy one. And he paid a price. His car, though clean and reliable, happened to be exceptionally slow. "It is mortifying," he wrote in March 1904, "to be making only ten to twelve miles an hour in an automobile, with horse-drawn carriages easily passing you, not to mention other kinds of automobiles."

"Get a horse!" I suppose people yelled at him, as they swept by in coaches and phaetons and broughams, the teams stepping smartly. What would they yell at me? Nothing, probably; they'd be going too fast. But derisive gestures wouldn't please me at all, nor would the sight of an electric car pulled over halfway up a mountain, with a generator snorting away behind it, do much to impress possible future converts.

But the third objection was the strongest. I was buying this car in order to have a pollution-free way of getting to class. I had rejected from the moment I heard of them the idea of getting one of the so-called hybrid cars that supplement an array of batteries with a small gasoline engine, so as to increase the range. (Not that I knew of any on the market. But prototypes exist, and they *will* be on the market. I could have waited.)

I meant to indulge a taste for purism. And the idea of buying gasoline in order to make electricity to charge the batteries to run the car did not appeal to me in the least. An emergency is one thing; a habit is another.

While I was still pacing around in front of Oliver's, unable to decide to go on, and unable to think of a reasonable alternative, a young man drove up with a truck full of bags of ice cubes. He delivered two bags to Judi, and then made a beeline for my car. "I've seen 'em on TV," he said, "but I never saw a real one before. Can I look under the hood? This is cool."

About fifteen minutes later he made the decision for me that I couldn't make for myself. He had meanwhile been all over the car—didn't waste any time asking about rainy days. He had told me about his part-time mechanic's job, had prophesied that in five years electrics will be common as blackberries, and had informed me that I hadn't even gotten to the hard part of Donner Pass yet. Now he told me what I should do.

"Go back to the fourth exit down," he said, "which is the town of Auburn. There's a U-Haul there, and a Ryder—and they have trucks just the size to carry a car. Rent one. Maybe you can get a drive-on, drive-off ramp, too. Load up, and you're on your way."

I couldn't have listened more receptively if I had been an early Greek consulting the oracle at Dodona. This oracle did, of course, tell me to use gasoline—but more efficiently than in the generator, and not to run the EV itself. I could regard it as a mere shipping device.

By now he was late on his delivery schedule, and he set off with his truck full of bags of ice cubes. Me, I felt so relieved to have a plan again, even if it was a plan to retreat, that I wound up enjoying the rest of my time in Meadow Vista. Soon I was talking to a retired electrical contractor named Jack MacKenzie. Jack was out for a Saturday morning drive in his 1932 Ford roadster. It made a pleasing sight. He had the body painted a burnt siena and the fenders painted black. He had the top down and the rumble seat open. Few post-World War Two cars have looked as good. "Hop in," he said, "and we'll take a spin."

By noon I had seen Jack's house and his five other cars, his two motorcycles and his camper. I had been safely returned to Oliver's and I had talked to five or six other customers. One of them, a lawyer from Sacramento, just up here for the weekend, was planning to call Solar Electric, with an eye to trying out an electric car herself. Sacramento is thirty feet above sea level, and natural electric car turf. Despite my own problems, I encouraged her.

The others weren't *that* enthusiastic, but each of them, like every other Californian who had come over to look at the car, had said something like "That's what we all need to do" or "No pollution. It's gotta happen." Several, of course, also asked about rainy days—and a perfectly natural question it is. If you know what solar panels are, and you see a car covered with them, which also has three signs on it, proclaiming its ability to get power directly from the sun, you may well think it gets all its power that way, not just 5 percent.

But mostly I heard "neat" and "cool" and "terrific." Nothing about "dumb idea" or "okay for Dodg'em cars." Either Californians are the politest of all Americans, or else there is a genuine and widespread interest in alternative vehicles.

These conversations did not use up the whole morning. I had also walked to a little lake half a mile below Oliver's, and climbed a hill half a mile above it, to get the view. I had bought and consumed Judi's largest size of popcorn. The car was still only half-charged—but Auburn is downhill, and I was tired of waiting. I got 149 miles toward home, and now I am going to back up about 10 miles and get ready to try again.

CHAPTER 6

Losing Ground

The electric vehicle was never intended for cross-country use.
—SHELDON SHACKET, *The Complete Book of Electric Vehicles,* 1979

AUBURN, CALIFORNIA, is an old gold-mining town, neatly bisected by I-80. It took about fifteen minutes to zip down there from Meadow Vista, and another ten to find the motel called the Auburn Inn, and to check in. Now I was only 138 miles from Santa Rosa.

"By the way, I'm driving an electric car. I'll need to plug it in to my room," I said to the desk clerk, as she handed me the key to 204.

She gave me a startled look. "You want to plug your *car* into your *room?* How would you do that?" I think she may have feared that I intended to drive right into the lobby and on upstairs, as the grandfather of a girl I once knew rode his horse up the front steps and into a brownstone house on East Sixty-fourth Street in New York City. (He was trying to impress the woman who later became Justine's grandmother.)

To reassure her, I went out and got one of my two fifty-foot orange cords. "I just need to run this out a window," I explained. "And of course, I'll be glad to pay for the electricity," I added, showing her The Letter.

She still looked dubious. "Just a minute," she said, and disappeared, presumably to consult someone.

"I'm afraid we can't permit that," she said on her return. "The manager's worried someone might trip on the cord. But he says you can park out back, and plug into the laundry room. There will be no extra charge."

That sounded fine to me. If I was losing ground, at least I was gaining rates. Tonight's room was down to fifty-one dollars, complete with a free meal for the car.

The Auburn Inn's laundry room has good circuits. I left the charger humming away at 14 amps, and went up to my room to call the U-Haul place. I got a rather brisk man. No, they didn't have a truck I could load a car into and drive to Vermont. They didn't deal in trucks like that, and no one else did, either. I must have misunderstood the person who told me they did. What they *could* rent was their smallest moving van plus a tow-dolly.

A what? A tow-dolly. This, he explained, was a two-wheeled affair that you hitched behind the van, and then you drove the front wheels of your car up onto it. But they didn't have any of those, either. They also had no small vans. "That's why we like you to reserve two weeks in advance," the man said. "That way we can give you what you want when you want it."

So to speak.

Ryder had nothing, either. So I called a place down the valley, two exits back toward Sacramento. I wanted a fourteen-foot truck and a tow-dolly to White River Junction, Vermont? Sure, the woman I talked to said. She did some quick figuring, and told me it would cost around $1,200. I would have nine days to get there.

If I had seen any alternative, I would indignantly have refused. Not only was I losing my adventure, I was going to be hustled along, and made to pay dearly for the privilege. But what else to do? Maybe I could get the car shipped, either by rail or in one of those car carriers you see on highways, though more likely not. Even if I could, I didn't want to. Sending it home like a UPS package would be the ultimate capitulation. This car and I were staying together.

I suppose there *was* a third alternative. Since I couldn't get over the mountains, I might consider going around them. A way exists.

When I first planned the trip, I heard about the southern route, which goes through Arizona and New Mexico and is said to be flat all the way. I never seriously considered it, because (a) I wanted to follow the route that Dr. Nelson Jackson and all those other gas car pioneers took in 1903, and (b) it seemed much longer.

Suppose I decided to adopt it now. What would I do? For starters, I'd turn around and drive back to Santa Rosa. Well, no. Probably I'd only have to retrace my course as far as Sacramento; it depended on how many mountains there were in the direct line between Sacramento and Los Angeles, and on this matter my maps were annoyingly vague. Either way, the second step would be to go south four or five hundred miles—certainly as far as Los Angeles and possibly to San Diego. Then finally I could point the car east and begin the trip. I'd still get home in 1991.

As well tell a salmon to swim back down the river and try the other branch. Every instinct I had said go east right now. I went out to the laundry room, unplugged, and drove off to pick up a van and dolly.

It took me a long time to find the rental place. I had imagined a big fenced yard full of trucks. What I eventually found was a small wooden office surrounded by no trucks at all. There were just two or three of those boxes on wheels that U-Haul rents. I got out and went into the office. The woman I had talked to was there.

"I'm the fellow who called about an hour ago. I don't see my truck and tow-dolly."

"You meant today?" she said, incredulous. "That's not how this business works. I thought you were comparing prices. I might be able to get you a fourteen-foot truck and a dolly by next Wednesday."

Back up to Auburn I drove, climbing and using juice all the way. I still wasn't detouring at the rate Dr. Jackson did in 1903. When *he* was near Sacramento, he reported, a woman from whom he asked directions deliberately sent him fifty-four miles out of his way "in order that her family might have the opportunity of seeing an automobile." This afternoon one of her great-grandchildren could see as many thousands as he or she pleased just by watching the flow on I-80 for a while.

At the inn I settled down on my bed with the phone and the yellow pages. Eventually—it would mean retreating all the way to Roseville—I managed to reserve a small truck and a dolly for Monday morning. From Roseville to White River Junction would cost me $1,286.

That settled, I could finally think about a very late lunch. Judi's popcorn had long since worn off. The question was where to get it.

Auburn is not a big town. In fact, by California standards it's tiny: 8,000, maybe 9,000 people. That's still big enough for it to exhibit what I believe is a common California pattern. The pattern runs thus. Start in the center, and you find a well-preserved nineteenth-century town. It will have a main street two lanes wide, with a handsome bank building, a nice old courthouse, an air of settled calm. Several other business streets and a dozen residential ones radiate off. They're narrow, too. There are lots of big old houses, some of them now split up into apartments. There's a pretty good café, with known and regular customers.

Surrounding this, like a patient with elephantiasis in arms, legs, fingers, and toes, is a region where every road is four lanes wide, except those that are six. The buildings are on the same scale. What in Vermont would be a drugstore is here something like an airplane hangar with resident pharmacist and shopping carts. What many places would be a parking lot is here an asphalt ocean, with clumps of stores dotted about like islands.

How, in a real ocean, do you go from one island to another? In a boat, of course. You'd probably drown if you tried to swim. So here. The asphalt ocean you navigate by car; you do not try to walk. And that explains why California is currently at the forefront of electric car development. If, in most urban parts of the state, you can't even cross the street without getting in your car, you had better have a car that is not too hostile to the environment. And you can't, as I was about to find out.

The Auburn Inn is on the north side of I-80, which here runs in a shallow trench. Most of the fast-fooderies in the elephantiasis zone are on the south side. So I thought: I'll just walk over and have lunch at one of those places I can plainly see across the road. It won't be scary, like Fairfield. I can also see the sidewalk.

It took me nine minutes to walk across the street. Even granting that I-80 is a pretty big street, this is too much. The actual distance was nothing: maybe 200 yards. Most of the time I spent waiting for permission to walk. Even to get on the cross street I had to find and push a dusty WALK button, wait about two minutes for anything to happen, then make one-half of a diagonal crossing. Then it was time to push another WALK button, and so on. All that for an inferior lunch.

There's a built-in contradiction to the system. Because in the elephantiasis zone the roads are so wide, the WALK signals have to stay on a long time. Otherwise a tottery old man or a mother with two small children couldn't get across. But while they (who aren't even here) are allowed their totter-time, traffic backs up—much of it, no doubt, people attempting to cross the street by car. WALK cycles must therefore be spaced far apart, or you'd have gridlock. Walking has now been severed from distance, tied to time, and made excessively difficult. Conclusion: Don't walk. And in fact, I saw only one other pedestrian, a morose teenager. That night I used my car to get to a restaurant, even though I was going less than a quarter of a mile.

On Sunday morning I used it again, much more willingly. I had a day to kill, a full charge, and a detailed map of Placer County, of which Auburn is the seat. My plans were first to get breakfast at some slow-food place in the center of town, and then to stroll. After that? I would let the day happen.

About 7:00 A.M. I got back on I-80, headed west. I now did the first completely stress-free driving of the trip. There was little traffic. I wasn't looking for motels or U-Hauls. Since I was only going one exit down, I couldn't possibly run low on fuel. Best of all, my body had begun to adapt to an EV. No longer did I have to concentrate on what to do with my hands and feet, or on what not to do with my eyes.

My hands had learned several things. One of the simplest was to treat the ignition key gently. When you get in a gas car, you first turn the key a little bit—and a number of dashboard lights come on (plus the radio, if a teenager was the last driver before you). Then you turn the key further. Your electric starter begins to make whiny, whirry noises and to crank your gasoline engine. Normally this soon roars to life, though sometimes not.

In an electric car you turn the key only that first little bit. The car is now ready to start. There's nothing further to do except step on the accelerator and go.

Another thing my hands had learned was to reach for the parking brake. They had actually learned this once before, when my father taught me to drive, forty years ago. But I'm afraid they quickly unlearned it again, once I had my license. Cars with combustion engines don't roll, not if you park on reasonably level ground and leave them in gear. It's better and safer, of course, to put the brake on; it's also slightly more bother. Just enough so that without ever making a conscious decision, I long ago ceased to, except on hills.

Electrics are sensitive to the slightest slope. In gear or not, they'll roll. Several times I had parked, gotten out—and seen the car quietly start off on its own. Alarming. By this fourth day it was automatic with me to pull the brake firmly out—a renewal of good habits that has since carried over to the guzzler.

What my feet had learned to do was to stop pushing the clutch in all the time. People who've spent their lives in cars with automatic transmissions don't have this problem, but those of us who drive manual shifts all wind up with fast left feet. Without thinking about it, you push in the clutch as you slow down for a red light, a stop sign, a traffic jam ahead. A good thing, too. If you didn't, the car would first buck and then stall. And when you reach the light, you keep it in, so that your engine can continue to idle—pistons popping in and out, interesting gases coming out the tailpipe, but nothing being accomplished. I've seen the claim that 10 or 15 percent of urban air pollution is caused by idling car, truck, and bus engines. (Idling railway locomotives help, too. You can see them parked on side tracks, throbbing gently, lights on, idling away six gallons of diesel fuel an hour. I think that's even more than a parked diesel truck wastes.)

All this is very different in an EV. As you approach the red light, stop sign, etc., you take your right foot off the accelerator, and your engine simply shuts off. Stops. Uses no energy. The *car* keeps moving, on up to the light or sign, at which point you brake to a halt. You have never touched your clutch pedal, and you won't until and if you shift gears. What happens when the light turns green? Why, you step on the accelerator pedal, the engine springs to life, and away you go. An electric car is something like a cat that in a fraction of a second can go from being asleep on the front porch to hot pursuit of a robin on the lawn. A gasoline car, of course, is more like the sort of human being who needs to wash his face, maybe swallow some coffee, before he feels fully awake.

As for my eyes, I had now begun to train them to stay away from the green bars. After my scare the first day, I had gotten into the neurotic habit of looking down every few seconds to see what bar I was on now. I had a real compulsion to watch the green flashes, even though they always upset me. I know why they did, too. It's the quantum-jump effect. On a gas gauge, the needle goes continuously but imperceptibly down, somewhat as a person ages continuously but imperceptibly from day to day. But with the voltage gauge it's more like bang, you're ten years older.

The trick is not to keep peeking. A glance every few miles is plenty—unless, of course, you're down on yellow bar. For a little trip like this one to central Auburn, there was no need to look at all, and I didn't. I looked at hills instead. And, of course, the gauge was still on F when I parked on an almost empty, deliciously narrow High Street, pulled the hand brake tight, and got out to explore.

I soon found the pretty good café—in Auburn it's called the Edelweiss—and ordered a ranch breakfast. That means big. Good eggs, too. Then I strolled the quiet streets, jaywalking frequently, and getting a sense of a real place.

When I came back to my car, a studious-looking young man was waiting beside it. He was carrying a Sunday paper and a plastic bottle of orange juice. "Is that your car?" he asked. "Did you drive it all the way out from Vermont? I was wondering how much of its power it gets from the sun."

"Yes. No. Five percent," I said, though not quite that fast.

A few minutes later I was giving him an electric car ride home, and hearing about what he called his awakening. Not religious, environmental. It occurred quite recently, during a college chemistry course. A single assignment on air pollution struck him almost the way St. Paul was struck on the way to Damascus. Now he thinks about environmental stuff all the time. He told me he worked part-time delivering pizza, and was trying to persuade his boss to shift to delivery vans powered by natural gas.

"I live up there," he said at the final turn, pointing up a semiverti-cal road. "You can just drop me here."

"I can just take you home," I said. The hill was by far the steepest I had yet encountered, but the car scooted right up, and not at 4 mph, either.

From there I drove down to the Placer County Courthouse, on the steps of which a very large number of people were having a group picture taken. I had just finished giving a ride to a deeply tanned man wearing the cowboy hat his grandfather wore from Texas to California in 1907, and to his small granddaughter, when another man came running up. He had a brown beard, he was wear-ing a yellow T-shirt, and he seemed to be quite excited. "Stop!" he called. "We've got to talk. I have an electric car, too."

CHAPTER 7

An Adventure in Moving

A very handy, ingenious Fellow, who was a cooper by trade, but was also a general Mechanic; for he was dexterous at making Wheels, and Handmills to grind Corn, was a good Turner, and a good Pot-maker. He also made anything that was proper to make of Earth or of Wood.

— DANIEL DEFOE, *Farther Adventures of Robinson Crusoe*

BROWN-BEARDED JOHN FRATCHER was once a fireman in Cleveland, Ohio. On vacations he liked to go long-distance bicycling. Once he bicycled clear across the United States. Firemen have a strong collegial sense, and he often spent the night in strange firehouses. If the engines went out to a fire while he was there, he went, too.

In 1978 he left the Cleveland Fire Department. His eldest child couldn't seem to shake her asthma, and a doctor suggested that a different climate might help. The family decided to move to California.

There are two ways that people commonly deal with their belongings when they move. One is to let your wallet do the work. You call a moving company. They send a crew who come and pack everything up, load it in a van, drive it to the new location, unload it, submit a huge bill.

The other is to have what U-Haul calls an adventure in moving. You pack everything up yourself. You rent a van, drive it to the new place, carry everything in. You do all the work yourself, and you still have the van to pay for.

John Fratcher chose neither of these methods. He had what anyone would call an adventure in moving. He happened to know another Cleveland fireman who owned a small moving company on the side. This man was about to retire an old beat-up van—a big one, twenty-eight feet long—and replace it with a new one. John bought the old van for $4,000. He announced his intention of driving it, with all his worldly possessions inside, to Sacramento.

There are about 1,200 men and women in the Cleveland Fire Department, and most of them began to laugh when they thought of John heading west in a decrepit moving van. Someone organized a pool on how far he would get before his final breakdown. The farthest anyone predicted he would make it was to the Platte River in Nebraska.

When John and the moving van arrived in Sacramento, he first unloaded. Then he sold the van for $4,000 to a Sacramento fireman who was moving to Utah.

I knew none of this, of course, when that bearded man came running up to me in the streets of Auburn. Didn't need to. It was quite enough to learn that he owned an electric car for me to regard him much as one might, when in a tangle, regard an angel physically descending from heaven. Here is help beyond reason or expectation.

Certainly I never expected to meet a fellow EV owner in Auburn. EV owners are scarce. The first sixty years of my life I hadn't met any at all. In the past year and a half, actively looking, I had met two. One was Julian Wise of Maryland, who had a pair of them laid up in his backyard. (He had been the sales manager for Jet, and when that company changed hands and then folded, he got two cars instead of pay.) I'd had an interesting visit with Julian, but of course didn't get to do any driving.

The other I had met just five days ago, and that was Gary Starr. I had talked to Gary probably a dozen times during my two days of hanging around Santa Rosa—and the typical conversation lasted forty-five seconds. Gary is the sort of central figure whose attention three people are always trying to catch, each needing an instant decision on something that matters, and meanwhile there is someone else on the phone. It would not have occurred to me to ask him to take me out for a spin in his EV. So my entire experience was with my own car.

In no time the bearded man had introduced me to a somewhat younger woman named Jan, and the three of us were seated in another of old Auburn's restaurants.

"Tell me about your car," I said.

"Well, it's a 1980 Jet Electrica. I haven't had it since 1980; I just got it last year." He went on to tell me that it had been laid up (like Julian's pair), its batteries dead. He'd picked it up for $3,600, repaired the wiring, bought new batteries, got it back on the road. A typical John Fratcher activity. "Tell me where you got your car," he now said. "You never drove that out from Vermont? You must have got it here in California."

I needed no more invitation than that; in fact, I would have settled for much less. I told him the whole story of my attempt to go over Donner Pass, the retreat to Auburn, the arrangement to rent a Ryder truck in Roseville tomorrow morning. He winced at the price.

If he was going to do anything angelic, now was the moment. "Can you think of a better way to get the car home?" I asked hopefully. "You think maybe I could still drive it?"

"No," he said, "you don't want to go over Donner Pass in that. I don't think you want to go to L.A., either." Then, apparently changing the subject, he told me about his move out from Cleveland—and added that when his brother moved out a few years later he bought *two* old moving vans. Drove the first one out, went back and loaded up the other, and drove that out, too. He sold them both for what he paid.

By now I am looking like stout Cortez on the peak in Darién. My eyes are full of wild surmise. If they can buy used moving vans in Ohio and sell them in sunny California, I can certainly buy a used pickup truck in California, and sell it in cold Vermont. First, of course, having towed my electric car home behind it. California truck: It sounds good. There used to be a big used-car operation in Vermont called Carolina Cars. Go there, and you could buy all sorts of hard-driven and doubtless ill-maintained vehicles brought up from South Carolina. Some had dents, some had sick engines, most polluted like crazy. But buyers flocked in, because the Carolina cars had not one trace of rust. Neither will the pickup truck that in my mind I have already bought.

There is just one problem. I am not a skilled judge of used vehicles. In fact, not even a competent one. "I don't suppose you'd help me find a truck?" I say to John.

"Sure. We can do that this afternoon."

By now John and Jan have finished their first breakfast, and I my second. "Can I see your Electrica now?" I ask.

"Well, we don't have it here." He looks at Jan, and she nods. "Why don't you come on home with us? Then you can try my car, and I'll try yours. We'll look for a pickup. After that, Jan and I are going to a lasagna party, and you can come with us if you want. It's all car people." Talk about falling into luck.

"Give me time to check out of the Auburn Inn, and I'm coming," I said.

Coming where? To a suburb called Citrus Heights, right on the edge of Sacramento. They are not Auburnites. They drove up this morning because Jan wanted to go to an antiques fair. They came in the van John uses in his bedding business rather than in the Electrica because you never know what you may take home from an antiques fair.

Right now they strolled off to a little more antiquing, and I raced back up to the inn to cancel tonight's reservation and to grab my stuff. Where will I spend tonight? Who knows? Who even cares? Then I started to race back down—still on I-80, of course. To my surprise I noticed that the road was climbing steadily uphill. Idiot! I have gotten on heading east. Perhaps it's the salmon instinct? If so, I'm right in the middle of a fish ladder, and can't stop. I have to climb up to a little town called Lincoln before I can get off, cross over, and start back down. What a waste of charge. And I'll be late besides.

But John and Jan have waited, and now they lead me twenty more miles back toward Santa Rosa. It's all downhill and easy; I still have two green bars left when they get off the great traffic river and lead me through Citrus Heights (which to my eye looks flat as a pancake). John's house, which, of course, he built himself, is in a section where there are still big lots and even bits of open land. His neighbor on the left is out in the bright sun, mounted on an old farm tractor, pulling a harrow around a huge vegetable garden.

John pulls up by his garage, and I pull up behind him, setting my brake firmly. "Pull up" is a curious phrase to describe bringing a car to a stop; it must be left over from horse days. I expect it was the reins you pulled up in order to make the horse stop. But considering my new brake habits, it fits the EV nicely.

John's first act is to go into his garage. He emerges holding one end of an electric cord even larger in diameter than the two Gary gave me in Santa Rosa. It's also shorter. Mine are both fifties, and this is a twenty-five. Since we are now in the tacitly admitted roles of car-master and car-student, he explains as he goes. "You want your charging cord heavy," he says. "At least fourteen gauge. The bigger it is, the more amps you can charge. And you want it short because you're losing a little power every foot."

"I've needed my whole hundred feet a couple of times," I say defiantly.

"Oh, sure. On your trip it makes sense to carry long cords. But when you get home, buy yourself a really short one."

He plugs me in. My car begins at once to take 16 amps.

Now we walk up beyond his garage. There sits a big brown car, an electric powerhouse with twenty-one batteries. It's one of three hundred that Jet built with Chrysler bodies. "Let's take a ride," John says.

We get in, he turns the key very slightly—and for the first time I see John Fratcher discomfited. Electric cars always start, I said. All you do is turn the key slightly. Almost always, I should have said.

John thinks a second, then opens the hood. Like my car, his has an array of six-volt batteries wired in series, and then one twelve-volter to run all the auxiliary stuff. "I bet it's that," he says. "It's the only battery I didn't replace when I got the car—they put it where it's just about impossible to get out."

He pulls the caps off and peers in. Yes, the electrolyte in the twelve-volter is way down. Casually, with the garden hose, he fills it. My mouth is wide open; I thought you always had to use distilled water. Actually, I still think distilled water is a good idea, but at least in Citrus Heights you clearly can manage with what comes out the tap.

We get back in, he turns the key, and away we glide. John drives the first several miles, and then he lets me take the wheel. I think my car may be slightly nimbler—but this car is plenty nimble enough to compete with the gas vehicles all around us.

There is one thing about John's car that I am already deeply envious of. The Jet has a running ammeter on its instrument panel. If you keep your eye on it, you can tell exactly how much electricity you are using at any given instant. Jam the accelerator down, and you'll see the gauge jump to 400 amperes. Coast up to a light, and you'll see that the motor is using no amps at all. What I'm especially struck by is how much difference driving style makes.

If I drive cowboy style, which you can do in an electric car—if I come up fast behind another car and then step on the brakes to avoid hitting it, if I pass, then come up fast behind another car, etc., the running ammeter jumps all over the place. It shows me using 70 amperes sometimes, 320 other times, quite a lot all the time. But if I drive a little more calmly, so that I glide up to lights and to other cars, not using the start-and-stop technique, the ammeter never goes over 100. Not here in level Citrus Heights.

The big difference in power consumption between calm driving and cowboy driving is not really news to me. Exactly the same difference applies to gas cars, and I've been hearing about it most of my life. Almost every magazine and newspaper in the country has at one time or another published an article called something like "Ten Tips for Good Driving." Tip Three, right after keeping your engine tuned and your tires properly inflated, is going to be: Avoid stop-and-start driving.

But in a gasoline car it all remains abstract. You can't *see* the difference in gasoline consumption, not while it's occurring. In John's car you can see the difference in electricity consumption every fraction of a second, and keeping the needle from leaping up becomes a kind of game you play with the car, just as you might play with a Nintendo or a pinball machine. John says it has had such an effect on him that he now even drives the van differently. Going through pretty countryside, you might not want to watch the needle all the time, any more than you'd want to stare at the green bars. But here on city streets, needle-watching makes the trip more interesting, not less. Logical or not, I feel myself the passive victim of the voltage gauge, but the active controller of the running ammeter.

When we get back from our ride, we unplug my car and go out again. "It handles nicely," John says after he's driven the Solar Electric a mile or two, and I bask in this praise from the car-master. I also like it, when we get back and raise the hood, that John notices and comments right away on how easily *my* twelve-volt battery could come out. He tests several of the batteries with a big hydrometer he produces from the garage (I want one, too) and pronounces them perfect. They should be, of course; this is only their fourth working day.

Now we go into the house. While Jan shows me her morning's haul—a handsome old perfume bottle, a pair of comic china pigs with wiggily heads, an antique black hat—John gets the Sunday paper and begins to call people with used pickups to sell. Older used pickups. "For what you need, you shouldn't have to spend more than three or four thousand," he says.

But most of the people with older pickups for sale are not home. Why should they be on a beautiful Sunday in May? They're out jamming the roads of Sacramento. The two who *are* home have already sold their vehicles. Probably I should worry. I still have the $1,286 van reserved for tomorrow morning, plus what is obviously the last available tow-dolly in Northern California. But here with the car-master I simply don't. Something will turn up.

CHAPTER 8

The Car Party

According to some child psychologists, today's children can make the vroom sound of a motor before they can form the word mamma.
—WOLFGANG ZUCKERMANN, *End of the Road: The World Car Crisis and How We Can Solve It,* 1991

SOME PEOPLE play bridge when they go to parties. Others watch TV, talk politics, roll back the rugs and dance. At the small party John and Jan took me to, we talked cars.

John told me what to expect (besides lasagna) as we drove over in the Electrica. "This isn't exactly a club meeting," he said, "but it sort of is. There'll be about a dozen people there. What we all have in common is, we all like Fords. Especially Falcons. What we like best are the sixty-fours."

John turned into a narrow street, quite unlike those ringing Auburn, and pulled up in front of a house set close to the road. A big red convertible, waxed and shiny, sat across the street, giving off an aura of power. Four men stood around it. "Ha," said John. "That's the central group right there."

We walked over to the convertible—a 1964, of course—and John introduced me to the four men. One was our host, a deeply tanned middle-aged man in shorts named Ron Wilson. "I hear you've got an electric car, too," he said. "It was a Ford, right? How do you like it?"

The second, somewhat younger, had a fine pure West Virginia accent, and the hands of someone who has held a lot of wrenches. His name was Larry Rowan. "Where the hail you find these people?" he said to John, giving me a smile so genuinely friendly that it felt like a welcome to the party, the day, quite possibly to life itself.

The other two men looked like California surfers. They were both young, tall, blond, long-haired. "Hi, howya doing?" said the one with curlier hair, whose name was Kern. I figured him for a student taking his time getting through some junior college. The fourth, another John, just smiled and shook hands. Probably at the same college, I thought.

"Come on in," said Ron, and led us through the house and into a remarkable backyard. On the left side was a swimming pool. A pretty young woman and her small daughter were busy skimming leaves off it. This was Melanie, Kern's friend, and her daughter, Ashley.

On the right side of the yard there was a stretch of grass. Behind that grew several spectacular trees. They were full of roses. Red roses peeped through the foliage and glowed along the branches, way up in the air. I had never seen any rose trees before. I had, of course, read about them in *Alice in Wonderland,* but as I clearly remembered from Sir John Tenniel's illustrations, those rose trees were tiny—no higher than the playing-card gardeners who tended them. These were tall trees.

I had to walk almost over to them before I realized that the trees were just some regular western species, and the roses, like vines, had simply climbed twenty feet up them. That walk across the yard also led me over to what from the swimming pool had seemed to be some green mounds near the rose trees. As I got nearer, I could see that they were actually piles of car parts, lightly grown over with shrubbery. I could see bumpers, fenders, assorted motor parts, a whole door. Since Ron and Larry had set a joking tone to the conversation, I figured I was free to wonder out loud if old radiators and clutches made good fertilizer for roses. Ron smiled.

"The problem with this yard isn't the roses, it's the swimming pool," he said. "It takes up too much room. What I figure is, I'll drain it and put in a two-bay garage. I'll finally have decent-sized grease pits."

"You are not going to touch that pool," said his grown daughter, also in the car business. "You're disgusting."

"Well, what about Kern's cars in his yard? Why don't you pick on him?" Ron asked.

Kern looked up. "Yeah, what about my cars?"

"He's got twenty-seven of them in his yard," Larry explained to me. "Real old junkers. He's always in trouble with the city."

"You mean his yard where he *lives?*" I asked.

John Turk laughed happily. "Where he lives. We haven't got any more room down at the shop; it's packed solid with cars there, too."

"Whoa," I said. "What shop?"

Then I learned about J & K's Mustang Parts and Body Shop, of Date Avenue, Sacramento. J was John Turk, K was Kern. They were actually both twenty-nine years old, and they had owned a business together since they were nineteen. Ron and Larry worked for them. Surfers, indeed. Autoholics and workaholics.

John Fratcher had meanwhile spotted his opportunity. "Maybe we can clear out a little space for you," he said to Kern. "This guy needs a pickup. Have you got one he could tow his electric car over the Sierras with? Tow right to Vermont, I guess. That right, Noel?" I nodded.

"Sure," said Kern. "We've got a Toyota four-wheel-drive. Took it in a couple of weeks ago. Fifty thousand miles."

"Can I see it?" I asked.

"Let's go," said Kern.

And so, on the afternoon of the quiet day I was going to spend in Auburn, I got in a bright red 1964 Falcon convertible, and went to Sacramento. Melanie and Ashley came along for the ride, and John Fratcher came in his role as car adviser to eastern visitors.

Kern drives fast. In fifteen minutes we were on Date Avenue, and he was unlocking a gate in the chain-link fence that encloses J & K's Mustang Parts. To one side of the building was a narrow alley full of tires, transmissions, puddles of transmission oil—and, parked at an incredibly steep angle, a tan Toyota truck. The bed was full of auto parts.

It turned out to be a 1981 truck, and obviously it may have had

150,000 rather than 50,000 miles on it. But 1981 four-wheel-drive Toyotas are something I know a little about, since I used to own one. Had it for seven years, until I got the present guzzler. This one looked like a fine healthy little truck. Kern watched placidly while I tried the lights (they all worked), put it in and out of four-wheel-drive, looked to see if there was a jack. (There was.) "Can I try it?" I asked.

When Kern had unloaded the auto parts, I got in and turned the key. A double turn, of course. The engine started right up. John came with me while I went to fill the truck with gas and take a little test drive. "What do you think?" I asked the buyer of moving vans.

"I think it's a good truck," he said. "I think it will get you home."

Back at J & K, I bought it. Paid $3,500. More accurately, I agreed to. It was a handshake contract: no papers, binders, or notaries. Then we all went back to Ron's for lasagna and car talk.

Before we left the party, I discussed timing with Kern. Part of our deal was that he'd check the truck out, and make sure it could really go 3,000 miles pulling a heavy electric car. He also needed to get hold of a new rear bumper, mount that, and then install a tow-ball for the tow-dolly.

"I suppose we should figure on Tuesday rather than tomorrow," I said reluctantly. I was itching to start up Donner Pass.

"It *would* be a little easier," he said.

Back at John's house, I unplugged my car and got ready to go. "Where are you going to spend the night?" John asked.

"I don't know yet."

"Well, I don't see any point in spending a lot of money on a bed. There's a real old-fashioned motel about three miles from here. It's a little run-down, but it's all right." He gave me directions.

"And what about tomorrow?" he asked as I finished writing down the directions. "There's a rail exposition in Sacramento—lots of steam locomotives. You might want to go to that."

I do like steam locomotives, but I've also seen a lot of them. I had never seen a John Fratcher before. "I'd rather spend the morning with you," I said. "Maybe I could be your assistant bed deliverer." He said tomorrow it would be just mattresses, and yes, I could. He'd pick me up at 9:00.

The Ranch Motel I found easily. It consisted of two rows of joined cabins, looking at each other across a rather nice grassy court with two sycamore trees. No roses in them. No paint on the cabins, either, or at least none since 1964 Fords were new. But it was thirty-three dollars a night, the kind of price I like. When I offered the manager an extra five dollars for two days' worth of electricity for the car, she waved it aside.

Once installed in No. 7, I did find a few problems. The mattress was definitely not one of John's; it had had years and years of hard service. There was no phone, so if I wanted to call my wife back in Vermont, I would have to use an open-air pay phone so sited that it picked up street noise splendidly. Most serious of all, I didn't see how I was going to charge the car. It had a half-charge from John's garage, of course, but tomorrow after mattress delivery I wanted to use it freely, and for that I wanted full charge.

Since there was a screen nailed on the one window, my first thought was to bring the cord in through the door. But fourteen-gauge is thick stuff, and the door won't shut all the way with the cord passing through. I wish to shut and lock it tonight. Locking is not something I usually think much about, but in the next two cabins to the left are a pair of young couples who have drunk too much, and who keep going in and out of the two rooms. One of the two men has a temper, which he has already lost twice in the little while I have been there. I don't want him pushing my door open by mistake. It might produce an interesting encounter, but I'd as soon not find out.

Fortunately, the same person who didn't paint the cabins also didn't nail the screens in very well. The nailheads protrude enough so that without a hammer and without damaging the screen in the slightest, I am able to get one corner loose and slip my cord through. Using my light bulb adapter on the historic old bedside lamp (that still leaves me a ceiling light), I easily plug in.

It's not an especially restful night. Someone—I assume Mr. Foul Mood—chooses the middle of it to do a repair on his car, something that requires a lot of hammering on metal. No doubt his real purpose is to annoy one or more of his companions, and annoying people like me is just an accidental by-product. But I have the car charging, I have a deal for a truck, I have a plan to get home. Nothing can upset me much.

CHAPTER 9

Solo Gets a Name

White had bought himself a Model T Ford roadster,
which he had christened "Hotspur."
—SCOTT ELLEDGE, *E. B. White: A Biography*

We took a room at the Lafayette and led Hotspur to a
fashionable garage. It was the first time the little fellow
had been among other cars in so long that he was
much embarrassed.
—E. B. WHITE, 1921

EARLY ON MONDAY MORNING I called the rental place to say I
would not be needing the truck. I still wanted the tow-dolly,
but I couldn't pick it up this morning, because I didn't have
anything to tow it with. (The electric car was plenty strong enough,
but it didn't have a hitch.) I'd be over for it tomorrow.

"All right," said an airy voice. "I'll tell him when he gets in."

Good. Everything was set. Now I just had a day to enjoy. John
would be coming at 9:00.

Delivering mattresses is not in itself wildly interesting, though
the glimpses of other people's houses you get sometimes are. John's
store was another matter. The building had spent many years as a
branch of the Bank of Italy, back before that grandiosely named
California institution became the Bank of America, and back before
branch banks began to copy the architecture of drive-in restaurants.
This branch was slightly decayed Spanish colonial, and John had (of

course) fixed it up. He had the ground floor filled with bedding, including some in the big old walk-in safe. Upstairs Jan ran a separate store called Petticoat Junction. It was highly specialized. She sold clothes to wear to square dances. There were lots of gingham dresses hanging about, lots of what I think is called froufrou. The store wasn't open this morning, and all those silent clothes produced a somewhat eerie effect. I half expected the whole place to come to life. The dresses and petticoats would begin to stir, and then to dance, and then the music would start—probably Aaron Copland's *Billy the Kid* suite.

Before John dropped me back at the Ranch Motel, he took me with him to a much less dreamy store, one that sold secondhand tools—thousands of them, better tools at better prices than any K Mart or Wal-Mart ever dreamed of. Being old, they were mostly even American-made. While he negotiated for some kind of complicated power grinder, I bought a few simple tools that I thought would be good to have on the trip. With two vehicles, weight limits no longer applied. I could even have gone back to the Napa Valley and bought my wine. What I did buy was a light hammer that would have loosened last night's screen in two seconds, a couple of screwdrivers, and a set of wrenches. And, at an auto supply house John also took me to, a hydrometer exactly like his. That is, top quality.

In the afternoon I went electric car exploring. Two especially nice things happened. The first took place in the big shady parking lot of a branch of the Sacramento Public Library. I had hardly stopped and pulled the brake up before two young guys turned round and came over to see the car. Neither was shaven. Neither looked particularly clean-cut. The taller and older one was wearing one earring—and I'm not sure what that means in Vermont, let alone Sacramento.

"Howdy," I said as they came up. I often put on a sort of false folksiness in situations like this. It's not deliberate; I just open my mouth and hear something folksy come out.

"That's quite a car," said the older one. "Could we take a look at it?" He put the electronics textbook he'd been carrying down on the curb, and stuck his head almost into the engine.

This branch library has a really huge parking lot, which was nearly empty, because today was Monday, and the library was closed. It's arranged more as a series of tree-bordered pools than as one big ocean. I wound up giving those two young men a short EV ride—not on the humming avenue out front, but through the parking lots. And then the astonishing thing happens. The taller, older boy says he owns a car radio store in the Bay Area. The other boy works for him. If I were to come down there with the electric car, he would install a new radio free, just because he likes the idea of electric cars so much. He gives me his name, which is Launce, the name of his store, and the phone number. That may have been mere politeness I encountered up in Meadow Vista, but when people start offering you free radios, I think you have to take their interest seriously. I also think that the image I had of California as lotus land is proving entirely false. On the contrary, maybe the state needs to look to its child labor laws. I keep meeting proprietors who started in business as teenagers.

The second encounter was in front of a mini-mall on Greenback Avenue. A young woman was using a pay phone when I drove in and parked about twenty feet away. At first she stayed on the phone, and divided herself between asking me car questions and giving the person on the other end a running account. "He's got solar panels *all over* the top," she'll say into the phone, and to me she'll call, "Can you drive on rainy days?"

But then she got so interested that she told her friend she was going to hang up and call back later. She came over to take a really close look. "I wish my husband was here," she said. "We've got a propane car, got it last year. But this is what *I* want."

Somewhat later that Monday afternoon, a third event occurred—but this one took place entirely in my mind. The car was fairly deep into Sacramento. I'd gone up a road called Winding Way to the vicinity of American River College, having noticed on a map that the street names in that vicinity were all academic. I thought it might amuse me to be at the intersection of Dartmouth Street and Vassar Street. In a mild way, it did. But now I was two blocks over, on the major thoroughfare called Auburn Boulevard, and rush hour had begun. My little EV was surrounded by what I suppose were really hundreds but felt like thousand of gasoline vehicles.

Quite suddenly it seemed to me as if the car were conscious of where it was—conscious and unperturbed. Even feeling jaunty. And then a second or two later I realized that this car was not an it but a he, and that his name was Solo. From alone in all that traffic, I suppose, with maybe a hint of solar energy as well.

I don't mean to be mystical about this. I don't really think the car named itself, or told me its gender. I think my subconscious was hard at work. But it did *feel* as if the car were deciding—and the more so in that it would never have occurred to my conscious mind that a car would be masculine. Surely cars have feminine gender. People *often* say, "Fill 'er up," when they are getting gas in those stations that offer so-called Full Service. I have never heard someone say, "Fill 'im up."

In any event, from that moment on I thought of the vehicle as a male car named Solo, and from here on I shall feel free to use his name.

At 8:00 o'clock Tuesday morning I packed up, tightened the screen in No. 7 with my hammer, and drove to J & K's Mustang Parts. The truck was entirely ready except for one detail. Kern had not mounted one of those round metal balls called trailer balls on the new rear bumper. He couldn't, he explained, until he knew what kind of dolly I had reserved, because different dollies take different sizes.

I sat in the little office at J & K, and called Roseville. This time I got the owner.

"You!" he said, in a distinctly non-airy voice. "You call on Saturday, and reserve a truck and a dolly for Monday morning, and I hold them for you. On Monday you call and cancel. Now you call and say you want the dolly, after all. It went out yesterday, Jack."

"What do you think I should do now?" I asked Kern, who was lying under a car.

"That was Ryder? You better try the main U-Haul office in Sacramento. Don't phone. You better just go."

The main U-Haul office in Sacramento is impressive. This is no filling station with a rental sideline. This is a place with an eight-bay garage where U-Haul trucks get serviced, teams of mechanics, an acre of paving. One thing they don't have, though, is a dolly. If they had had, it would have been $350 for Vermont.

"Try ABC," a pleasant young clerk advises. ABC has one, but they won't rent it one-way. Try Ryder, their clerk suggests.

Around 10:30 I am back at the big U-Haul place to see if they might have that more modest piece of equipment, a tow-bar. They do not rent tow-bars, but maybe Glen out in the garage has one he can sell me.

"What are you going to tow?" Glen asks. His eyes light up when he sees the pretty little electric car, and his protective feelings are aroused. "I wouldn't do it, if I were you," he says. "How're you going to attach the tow-bar to the car? We'd have to install a couple of plates under the front that would make the car at least forty pounds heavier. You don't want to do that."

True. I don't. But I do want to resume my journey. It comforts me not at all to think that Dr. Jackson and Sewall Crocker spent nineteen of their sixty-five days going nowhere, waiting one place and another for new parts to be shipped by rail, or for a local blacksmith to make them a part. It comforts me even less to think that eighteen of those nineteen days were west of Omaha.

"Glen, I've looked all over Sacramento for a dolly. There aren't any. I want to order a tow-bar."

"It's your car. Okay, I'll order it this morning, and we should have it in a week."

The whole day went like that. Kern, seeing no other way to get rid of me, eventually took up the case himself. In midafternoon he located an actual dolly on the other side of Sacramento, and he and Melanie and I drove over to get it. The garage man, a friend of Kern's, is all smiles when we arrive, deeply embarrassed two minutes later. "I can't believe it," he says. "The computer showed I had two—and they both went out this morning."

Kern rapidly drove ten miles back across Sacramento to an RV dealer he knew, and for $120 this man reached up on a rack and handed me a tow-bar. Then he passed over a matching trailer ball. That took care of the truck end. There was still Solo to prepare, since it's now clear he won't be riding graciously with his front wheels up on a dolly. Back on Date Avenue, Kern persuades a friend with a welding shop to drop what he is doing and weld two "ears" on Solo's front bumper. These are what the tow-bar will attach to. My car will now have ears for the rest of its life, of course—which is actually good. I may want to tow it again someday.

By 6:00 P.M. the welding is done, and John has mounted the trailer ball on the truck. He and Kern now help me hook Solo on behind the truck. It takes a good twenty minutes, since the spacing has to be perfect, and all these parts are brand-new, not yet broken in and comfortable. I don't think I could have done it alone.

You have to have working signal lights on a towed vehicle, and Kern now lends me a set of very fancy ones. They're magnetic. I can set them on the metal roof of my car—there is just room behind the last solar panel—and they will stay firmly in place. When I want to uncouple the vehicles and take the car out on its own, I just pluck them off. "Just mail them back when you get to Vermont," he says.

It has been a long, long day. Hot, too. Everyone but Kern and John has gone home. John now does the paperwork, while Kern wires those magnetic tow-lights into the truck's electrical system. I have called my insurance company back in New England, and the truck is covered. John tapes a bill of sale in the rear window of the truck. "Your California plates are good for thirty days," he says, "and we'll try to have the title for you when you get home." I write out a check.

Just before 7:00, my little caravan pulls out of J & K's Mustang Parts, headed once more toward Donner Pass. For four days I have been stalled in my trip—except when I was going backward—and it has been a frustrating time. I have known farmers back in Vermont who bought a fall calf to raise. One way to do that is to keep the calf tied in the barn until spring. Its movements are limited to what it can do while tied to a six- or seven-foot rope. When the calf is untied in the spring, and turned out in the barnyard, it is apt to go almost crazy with joy. It will leap, bound, caroom off the cows, run in circles around the barnyard as many as thirty times without pausing.

I feel like such a calf.

CHAPTER 10

The Nevada Motel

With the growth of suburban centers and with the increase of travel by automobile, a form of transient hotel, called a motel, became popular. Situated on or near a highway, and usually beyond the limits of the nearest city, motels became increasingly elaborate and successfully rivaled luxury hotels.
—*The Columbia Encyclopedia,* entry "hotel"

AN HOUR after leaving J & K, I again approached Meadow Vista. This time I kept going, on up Donner Pass. Very soon I-80 narrowed to two lanes in each direction. Not too long after that, the first bits of snow appeared. Almost simultaneously, I shifted into second gear.

For the second time in a week, I was learning a new way of driving. A 1981 Toyota pickup held no surprises, of course. But that same pickup pulling an electric car did. What such a rig amounted to was a miniature trailer-truck, and I was already beginning to think like a truck driver.

To begin with, I was freeing myself of road-guilt. What's road-guilt? The feeling you get if you are pottering along at the speed limit, or a little slower, and there are a bunch of cars piled up behind you, dying to get by, dying to go faster. I have often speeded up, even though I was maybe looking for a street address or worrying about cops, so as not to keep blocking them. Occasionally, on curvy roads where it's hard to pass, I have even pulled over.

But as a truck driver you can't always be so obliging. Take the present moment. Like the big semis, I was pulling up Donner Pass with the accelerator pushed to the floor, going thirty-five miles an hour in third gear, and shifting down into second for the worst bits. The road was full, and there were cars behind me in the right lane that had to wait fifteen or even thirty seconds to swing around. I felt no guilt. I couldn't possibly have speeded up. As for moving out on the shoulder and losing half my momentum, get real. No, fast, impatient cars in my lane would just have to find their own way past. We trucks are doing all we can.

Another thing I was learning was to think before I stepped on the brakes. Truckers must. If you're driving a forty-ton, three-piece truck, you do not stop on a dime, or even a fifty-cent piece. Air brakes and all, you need room. Which means you have to have your strategy clearly in mind as you approach a light, or an interstate exit, or a car in front of you that is rapidly slowing down because the occupants have seen a deer grazing off to the right.

Me, too. I needed a strategy. My miniature tractor-trailer, to be sure, weighed only about three tons—but it was still hard to stop. It had no air brakes, nor any way of using the brakes of the EV. Everything depended on the ordinary braking power of one small Toyota pickup—and as I learned within thirty seconds of leaving J & K, that power was limited. When I came to the end of Date Avenue, I very nearly went right on through the stop sign, there was so much weight behind, urging me forward.

Dealing with the brakes was not much of a problem here on the long climb up Donner Pass, but part of my mind was already thinking with interest how it would be going down the other side.

But my real, serious truck-thoughts were reserved for the matter of backing up. You can't do much backing with a trailer-truck. You can't do *any* when you're pulling another vehicle with a tow-bar. At least, not the kind I bought. "Do Not Back Up," the makers had stamped right in the metal of the bar, and they had also blazoned this on a yellow warning sticker. I wasn't sure how literally to take them. If they meant don't turn the wrong way into a one-way street, go half a block, and then try to back out, pushing the other vehicle, fine. If they meant don't park the rig in someone's driveway and then try to back both vehicles out onto the street, fair enough. These are restrictions one can live with.

But if they meant don't back up at all, not even ten feet, why, then your freedom as a driver is just about gone. You're a little hungry, and you see a place to stop for coffee and a Danish? Forget it; you won't be able to get out of that row of angled parking spots in front of the café.

It's evening, and you see a motel. Unless you also see a complete circular drive, with parking permitted along the sides, keep going.

Here's a pretty little town, with a row of really nice old brick houses and an interesting church. Shall we stop? Sorry, parallel parking on the main street is out of the question—unless we happen to find four empty spaces in a row, in which case we can angle in through the first one, park our two vehicles in the second and third, and emerge headfirst through the fourth. Provided no rat has taken it meanwhile.

Naturally I had asked Kern what he thought the warning meant. Would it really be so awful to back up just a little, just enough to wiggle out of places? The big trucks do it. "You probably can, a few times," Kern had said, "and then you'll start jamming up the tow-bar." Great. Stuck in the middle of Wyoming with a jammed tow-bar.

All this thought was giving me new insight, not only into the lives of truckers (drivers is what they actually call themselves), but also into the reason why truck stops exist. Basically, a truck stop is a place where you never have to back up. Since possibly I never could, I decided I would look for truck stops, and when possible spend my nights at them. Some have motels; some don't.

By now I had crossed the pass, and was going down the other side in third gear, headed for Truckee, California, and then the Nevada border. It was dark now; I could just see glimmers of snow until I got down too low again. Here was my plan. Naturally I had no idea where any truck stops were, except the one back in Fairfield, where Jason's café and all the telephones were. Neither maps nor AAA guides say much about them. But as soon as I got to Nevada, I would start looking. Why not now? Because I was determined to leave California tonight. The salmon in me said it was essential.

As I well knew, the first town you hit in Nevada is a place called Verdi. The name amused me. I'll just go to Verdi, I thought. If there's a truck stop, wonderful. If there isn't, maybe I can find a motel with a circular drive, or with a huge empty parking lot out back. I'm not unhitching tonight. Why risk it? It took Kern and me twenty minutes working together, to get the two vehicles attached. What if one person can't do it at all?

All Verdi had, that I could see in the dark, was a couple of brightly lit casinos. So I went on the eight miles to Reno, driving a steady 50 mph, as I had ever since the road leveled off and I came out of third gear. I was scared to go faster. Whenever I tried it, the truck would begin to wobble. It was probably too light to be pulling not just a car but half a ton of extra batteries.

When I got off I-80, tapping my brakes carefully, and drove into Reno for gas, I quickly discovered that I'd just as soon spend the night in Gomorrah. I felt somewhat the way a new steel ball does when it is first shot into a pinball machine. All those buildings outlined in neon! All the flashing lights, the urgent noises, the cacophony of colors. I couldn't wait to get back on I-80 and into the dark Nevada night. My new revised plan was to get so far beyond Reno that I couldn't possibly even see it as a glow on the backward horizon, and then to look for a rest area to spend the night in. My maps showed one this side of Winnemucca. It would mean another 150 miles of driving—but the salmon feeling was strong.

Midnight on I-80 is pleasant in Nevada. There are no more cars out. A big truck thunders past only once every minute or two, making a shock wave in the air and causing the pickup and the EV to rock slightly. Everything is dark and peaceful. Every half hour or so I passed a power plant glowing with lights or a small town glowing with casinos. Reno overdoes it with the lights, but a little town like Lovelock really does look like a jewel against the desert.

I never got to the rest area at Winnemucca because about 1:30 in the morning I saw a jewel-glow on the left, and it turned out to be the Burns Brothers truck stop in Mill City. (This is a city the way Walden Pond is an ocean.) I drove cautiously down the exit ramp, still nearly overshooting it, into the truck stop, and parked my little rig at the end of a row of giant trailer-trucks. Then I walked into the one immense building that houses everything. There was the casino—I think it's probably illegal in Nevada to have even a village without a casino—and there were the store, the restaurant, the phone room, the motel.

Things were still hopping at 1:30. Scores of truckers were in the restaurant and the casino. There was loud conversation, louder music. All that blaze of lights outside. No sleep for me, I thought. But here I was, and I registered anyway.

Along with my room key, the clerk gave me a card something like those mileage things airlines have. If I stay ten times at a Burns Brothers motel, the eleventh night will be free. She also gave me a chit for a free drink in the casino, and another chit for a free roll of nickels. A third one cut a dollar off the price of whatever I decide to have for breakfast in the morning. One more chit, and they'd be paying me to stay there.

Now the clerk points me toward the motel part of the building. I go through a heavy door—and suddenly I am in a hushed corridor, with good insulation and thick carpet.

I enter my room. It is the nicest motel room I have ever been in. What do you generally find in a motel room? Two double beds, horrible wallpaper, a mean little bathroom. Often the bathroom has some sort of patent light switch that also controls a noisy exhaust fan. Unless you want to grope in the dark, you're compelled to run the fan, waste energy, hear the noise.

This place is different. The first thing I notice is that the room is huge—when I measure it in the morning, it turns out to be fourteen feet by twenty. There's no wallpaper at all, just a clear fresh off-white paint. There is one bed; it has an oak headboard.

I go into the bathroom and I almost gasp. Mondrian could have designed it. It's all clean surfaces and good angles. A ten-foot counter runs along one side. No need to put your shaving stuff on top of the toilet *here*. Halfway down the counter is a sink, and over the sink a big rectangular mirror. I measured that the next morning, too. It's five feet long, three feet high.

Even the guest toiletries are different. You know what motels usually offer: a tiny plastic bottle of shampoo, a disposable shower cap, two little bits of wrapped-up soap about the size of matchbooks.

Burns Brothers doesn't bother with shampoo, etc. They do give you two serious bars of soap—say, four times as big as the motel norm. Clearly when a driver takes a shower, he wants a piece of soap big enough to find again.

Back in the room, I look around again. Whoever designed it knows something about public decoration. There's no Van Gogh print on the wall, no phony fox-hunting scene. Instead, there's a pretty good print of a painting by the American artist Thomas Moran (1837–1926). It shows an Indian camp at Green River, Wyoming. It was just right. So was the view of Nevada mountains I got out my window the next morning. (With, admittedly, a number of large trucks in the foreground.)

Why, you may wonder, is everybody so good to truckers? Phones at Jason's, rolls of nickels here. The answer is simple. For the same reason everybody is good to Rockefellers and du Ponts. They have money to spend. When a trucker stops at a truck stop, one thing he does is to get more fuel. If he's only down halfway, he might buy only 150 gallons. If he's really low, he'll be pumping more like 275. That's business worth having. The motel, the free showers, the telephones—they're like the nectar flowers put out to attract butterflies.

Next morning I settle up my bill. The room has cost me $21.35, Nevada tax included. I am stunned. The best motel room I have ever stayed in is also the cheapest.

By 9:00 o'clock I am on the road again. It's a cool, cloudy day. The worst of the salmon fever has abated, now that I'm 160 miles or so into Nevada, and heading east at my steady 50 mph. The truck continues to weave a little when I go even slightly faster. I get an idea. Not many miles past Mill City, the road climbs over a pass, and up at the top there's a considerable rubble of rocks lying on the ground. It's a rather ugly conglomerate, yellowish brown, but I'm not going to be choosy, as I would when building a stone wall at home. I pull over, get out, and find two rocks the right size. That is, as big as I can conveniently lift—90 or a 100 pounds each. I put them in the truck, up front, on the floor of the passenger side. I pause a minute to look ahead at the view of a sagebrush valley, get back in, and go my way.

The difference is apparent at once. With the stone passenger, I can cruise at fifty-five. Occasionally, if I see no risk of either having to use my brakes or going down a hill, I edge up to sixty.

The electric car continues to interest people, even though it's now being towed. (Most people assume I'm taking it to a show.) Back at Burns Brothers this morning, an elderly couple from Oregon spent about ten minutes studying the car and laughing at the little joke that Solar Electric played when they converted it. The car used, of course, to have a gas tank. It still has the little flap on the right rear fender that would lift if you were going to pump gas. Only now, if you lift it, you see a three-prong electric plug. It's to that I attach my cord when I'm charging.

"I wish they'd hurry up with electric cars," the wife says, still laughing. "I want to live long enough to own one."

And now, in early afternoon, I am at Geyser Peak rest area, looking at the mass of tumbleweed piled up against a barbwire fence when a man in a black cowboy hat leaps out of a big RV and comes over to examine my solar panels. "Had to see these," he says. "The company I work for, we've got a solar division, and we ship a lot of panels to the Middle East. They use 'em to power water desalinization plants." Some people also use them to power the household appliances in an RV, but I failed to see if he had any on top.

That night I spent in Wells, Nevada, and still I hadn't unhooked Solo. But I mean to try soon. That was May 8, and in only six days my wife was flying out—we don't know to exactly where—to make part of the trip with me. This has been planned for months. Originally we expected to drive in the electric car together. Now, of course, one of us will be in each vehicle. By the time she comes, I will be in the level Midwest, and Solo can spurn tow trucks. But first I need the courage to uncouple.

CHAPTER 11

Scorn in Utah, Skepticism in Wyoming

The general public, however, still seems to think of EV's as slow moving impractical curiosities for eccentrics.

—PHILIP TERPSTRA, *Electric Vehicle Directory,* 1991

IT WAS SNOWING when I woke up. Two inches lay on the ground, and more big wet flakes were falling. Nevada looked its prettiest, this May morning. The landscape had a stippled appearance—white with green undertones. If Thomas Moran, that good painter, had been there all night with a big enough brush, I could imagine his having redecorated the whole state. The only thing he had neglected was to put in some movement, and that soon got remedied. Half an hour out, I came into Independence Valley, the last level place before the steep climb up to Pequop Summit. A long line of cows and calves were walking eastward in single file. There were at least 200 of them, moving parallel to the interstate, but on a path of their own, some fifty yards beyond the I-80 fence.

Looking through the snowy air, I recognized at least five breeds in the procession. Herefords predominated, but there were many other kinds and colors. All walking steadily east. I felt a sense of mysterious purpose, as if they were headed to some great cattle meeting, some initiation ceremony for the calves—or possibly to the last casino, in tiny West Wendover, just before the Utah border.

When I crossed into Utah, I entered a different time zone, and maybe also a different emotional zone. You might call it the poker-face zone.

With rare exceptions, such as the man having a cigarette by the Travelodge pool, my first night out from Santa Rosa, people on the West Coast had been openly curious about the electric car. They had also tended to like it, even give it a kind of environmental blessing. Now, in Utah, Solo became invisible. Or since a bright red car with solar panels on top and white lettering on the sides can't really be invisible, I should say that now it became etiquette to ignore this object rolling along behind the pickup truck. You wouldn't, if you were a Utahan, comment on an iguana I was out walking on a leash, and probably not if I had a turkey feather glued to each eyebrow, so don't say anything about the electric car, either. It's none of your business.

There were, of course, occasional people in Utah who openly noticed Solo and who came up and made comments. These comments tended to be very different, however, from those I'd heard in California and Nevada. They were apt to be derisive.

I had my first taste of Utah scorn not five miles from the border, in a filling station. I was getting oil *and* gas *and* water for the pickup; towing a car up Pequop Summit and then Silver Zone Pass takes a lot out of a little truck.

The very tall young man who pumped the gas stared back at the EV while perhaps five gallons went in the truck. Then he spoke. "That's electric?" he said. "It looks like a 1985 Ford Escort to me."

"Well, it was." I explained about the conversion.

"Do they give you the gas engine, too, just in case?" he asked, keeping his face perfectly straight.

"Nope."

"Can I ask how much it cost?"

"Seventeen thousand five hundred."

"Too bad you don't like gas cars. Around here you could get three 1985 Ford Escorts for that. Maybe four."

I paid, and got back in the truck. As I waited for a chance to pull out onto the street, he made one last remark. Presumably it was intended for me, though officially he addressed it to a teenage boy who was hanging around the station drinking diet soda. "I wonder," the tall pump-handler mused, "if we'll ever see an electric car towing a gas one."

Yes, wise guy, one day you will see that. And it won't be something new, either, but a second coming. Electrics fairly often towed gas cars back at the turn of the century, because gas cars fairly often broke down. Listen to the testimony of a New York doctor named George Sauer in the year 1903. Dr. Sauer, an automobile nut, first owned a steamer, then a gasoline car. By 1903 he had switched to an "instantly, silently, and fusslessly startable electric." Since buying it, he has been king of his part of Manhattan. "Frequently have we towed our friends, but we have never yet been towed."

And electric vehicles have more uses than that, wise guy. Once in the year 1901 all the lights failed in a church in Stratford, Connecticut, right in the middle of an evening service. What happened? Why, one member of the congregation happened to have come to church in her electric car. She backed up to the church, plugged the lights into her car, and the service resumed. Or think of Tiffany's in 1904. Tired of having its employees lug all the packages from all the floors down to street level, and then outside, to be loaded in delivery trucks, Tiffany's bought three "elegant electric vans." And then in its new building at Fifth Avenue and Thirty-seventh Street, the company installed a giant elevator. Electric vans could and did go right in the store (back entrance, I admit) and then ride the elevator, picking up packages on every floor. Try that with a combustion engine, wise guy.

Soon after I hit Utah, the snow turned to rain. When a man in Coalville told me the rain was expected to last all day and all the coming night, I gave up any thought of detouring south so as to look around the wild canyon country that Edward Abbey (my second-favorite western author) has written about. I would head straight on for Wyoming, and for the famous truck stop called Little America, which even has its own zip code.

Another hour brought me to Wyoming, still in rain, and two more to Little America, which is actually huge. A nice truck stop, too, though no threat to Burns Brothers in Mill City. (If you imagine a Christmas package with the wrapping paper on the inside, you'll have a pretty good idea of a Little America motel room.)

I had promised myself to start unhitching the car tonight, but there's really nowhere much to go from Little America—and besides, when I arrived at 8:00 P.M. the rain seemed to be turning back to snow. I phoned my wife instead. We had plans to make.

Each holding a phone in one hand and a map in the other, we worked out our rendezvous. It needed to be somewhere between a 1,000 and 1,500 miles ahead, and in flat country that would be a pleasure to drive through. We finally decided to meet at Peoria Regional Airport, in Illinois. We didn't even consider Chicago, 150 miles to the north, for reasons you can easily guess. A person who is made nervous by the thought of driving his electric car into a strange city no bigger than Fairfield, California, pop. 80,000, is going to experience something close to panic at the prospect of towing that car into the Chicago metropolitan area, pop. 8 million. I would bet anything you have to back up to get out of parking places at O'Hare Airport.

We did consider several other small airports, such as the one that serves Davenport, Iowa, but Peoria seemed to lead on to the most appealing roads. In particular, a two-lane road called Illinois 24, and later Indiana 24, goes straight east from Peoria for several hundred miles, through lightly settled country. Our maps showed plenty of little towns along 24, such as Gridley and Chatsworth, Illinois, and Albion, Indiana, but nothing large until the road finally curved north into Fort Wayne. It seemed like an ideal place for a carefree electric car drive. Provided Anne could get a ticket, we would meet in Peoria five days from now.

People in Wyoming, like those in Utah, are good at concealing interest. No one at Little America even glanced at Solo next morning, nor did anyone in the town of Rock Springs, where I stopped for a couple of hours when the rain finally ended. The red-haired boy who pumped gas for me in Rock Springs even managed to conceal any serious interest in his job. He was dreaming along with the nozzle in his hand when I heard that gurgly sound that means you're almost full, and then about a teacupful of gas splashed onto the ground. "I think it's full," I said hastily. But now, out of his trance, he was so intent on making the sale an even fifteen dollars that he managed to spill another cupful. A teacup holds six ounces—I just measured. So, twelve ounces of gas on the ground. Enough to take the truck two miles.

That encounter may have been atypical, though. I may have gotten closer to what Wyoming is like a few miles farther on, when I stopped at Bitter Creek rest area for the view. The minute I went in the building, I saw the great translucent southward-facing shutters of a passive solar installation. Next I read a big sign put up by the Wyoming State Highway Department. It not only explained how the shutters work to heat the building, but gave details on the earth berm, the thermal mass of brick, the solar panels on the roof that produce hot water for the rest rooms. Finally, I noticed a woman who worked there—she had a pipe wrench and was fixing a pipe—and started asking her questions. Thus I met Catherine Logan, who has managed the rest area for fifteen years.

"Yes, I like it," Catherine told me. "We save forty-five to fifty percent on the electric bills. And we don't get frozen water pipes any more."

"How often did you use to?"

"Every winter. We can get down to sixty below. They'd freeze right up on a day like that, if there was wind. The state put in the solar six years ago. Not one problem since."

Are there more rest areas like Bitter Creek? Yes, seventeen. "And there might be one that's wind power. I wouldn't swear. I haven't seen it."

Catherine turned out to be perfectly aware of my solar car parked outside—she just wasn't going to say anything. But now she came out and cocked an experienced eye at my panels. Then she pointed to a couple of oil wells in plain sight of the rest area, their black beaks dipping and dipping. "This is oil and gas country," she said, "but we don't use it right. There's a lot of things should be solar, and aren't. I like your car."

It was the best blessing so far.

That night I spent in Laramie, not isolated in a truck stop, but at the Laramie Inn, in the center of town. Since I was going to unhitch, I didn't need to give a thought to the size of the parking lot. I did, of course, need to get power, and the young woman at the desk readily agreed to my plugging in back at maintenance. No charge, she said—though when I checked out next day, a $2.50 charge had appeared. Obviously she got overruled.

Then I went out, and for the first time since Kern and I mated them in Sacramento, I separated the truck and the car. It was not hard. It did, however, reveal a brand-new problem. The truck, as I've mentioned, had California plates, said to be good for thirty days. License plates are no passion of mine, and I had barely glanced at them when I bought the truck. Since then I had become familiar enough with the front one, but the back one I hadn't seen at all, the view of it always being cut off by a bright red electric car. It was visible now, though, and what I saw stunned me. Unlike the front plate, the rear one had one of those annual stickers in the upper right-hand corner—and the sticker said "89." These plates were good for zero days.

As long as I kept towing, I'd be all right. Cops couldn't see the rear plate, either, just the fresh green Vermont one on Solo. But what would happen when Anne joined me in Peoria, and we started driving both vehicles? I had a moment of wishing for a nice legal Ryder truck.

Well, there was nothing I could do tonight. There were four days left to think of solutions. No point in spoiling my time in Laramie. Never mind plates: I would just check Solo's charge, and then be off to see the town. I turned the key slightly, and was instantly proud of my panels. The top green bar was gleaming. I hadn't plugged in since Citrus Heights, and a full half of the daylight time since then, it had been either snowing or raining. But 50 percent sunlight had been enough. I threw a suitcase in my room, then hopped back in the car and set off.

The University of Wyoming is the main thing in Laramie, and this turned out to be graduation weekend. One day later (today was Friday), and I wouldn't have found a room within thirty miles. There were plenty of seniors around, though, and just before dark, on Third Street, I met one. College seniors are exceptions to all rules, and this one came striding purposefully over to the car.

"Hi," he said. "I see you've got an EV. Could I ask you a few questions?"

"All you want."

Soon we were having a beer together, having driven to the beer place by electric car. By then I knew my student was named Rod, and that he was an intending environmental scientist.

"How much of the car's power comes from the solar panels?" Rod asked.

"About five percent."

"I figured it had to be less than a tenth. So where do you get the rest?"

"Right now, from the grid. But when I get home, I'll be making my own electricity. I have twenty-eight solar panels on the barn roof."

"Same size as on the car?"

"Bigger."

"You happen to know the measurements?"

"Sure. The four roof panels on the car are sixteen inches by thirty-seven inches, which comes out to just over four square feet of collecting area per panel. The twenty-eight barn panels can each collect sunlight from an area of about six square feet. They're at a better angle, too."

Rod gave me the sort of look that a customs official gives you when she has checked one suitcase, and tentatively decided that you are not trying to smuggle stuff, after all.

"Well, maybe your car is okay," he said. "And maybe I'm just paranoid. But a lot of us in Wyoming think that electric cars are just one more California rip-off scheme. You know, first they want our water, now they want our air."

I didn't pretend not to know what he meant. He was talking about California's new zero-emissions law. Starting in 1998, 2 percent of all the new cars sold in California have to be completely nonpolluting—which at the moment means they have to be electric. Over the next five years, that figure rises to 10 percent, which means that by 2003, around 200,000 electric cars a year will be sold in California. That's a market worth having—and that's what Solar Electric, and General Motors, and Ford, and the Solar Car Corporation of Melbourne, Florida, and Nissan, and the Swedish company Clean Air Transport are all thinking about.

But what people in Wyoming are thinking about—a few of them, anyway—is where the electricity to run 200,000 new EVs a year is going to come from. What they fear is that giant new coal-fired generating plants will be built well east of California—plants like the one that dirties the air of Grand Canyon right now. (You should hear Edward Abbey on the subject—and you will, if you read *Desert Solitaire* or *The Monkey Wrench Gang*.) That plant is owned partly by the U.S. government; it supplies energy to Los Angeles.

There is a piece of shorthand for this fear. The states of Colorado, Utah, Arizona, and New Mexico all come together at exactly 37 degrees north latitude and 114 degrees west longitude. The meeting place is as square and neat as a street intersection, and the spot is widely known as Four Corners. What many people in the Mountain West believe is that electric automobiles are simply a way for California to dump its polluted air at Four Corners.

Rod had obviously taken a course that went into these matters, or done some intensive reading on his own, because he had figures to quote. "I know the California Air Resources Board claims that electric cars will reduce pollution per vehicle something like ninety percent," he said. "Even counting what the power plant puts out. But that's bullshit. They may reduce it some, but what I hear is that EVs will be *worse* in terms of smog and effects on the ozone layer. Only, we get the smog, instead of L.A."

"The facts are hard to get at here," I said. "In fact, there really aren't many facts, there are mostly assumptions."

"But what *I* hear is that coal-fired plants could be a lot cleaner than they are, though there's no question they would still pollute. Still, I wouldn't be interested in electric cars if I thought they would have to get most of their power from coal-burning plants."

"But you don't mind nuclear?" Rod asked.

"I waver on that one. They certainly don't put much junk in the air. On the other hand, I can't ever forget that if nuclear power plants had come along in the 1930s instead of in the fifties and sixties, Hitler would not have hesitated to bomb the ones in England, and I'm not even entirely sure we would have spared the ones in Germany."

"So what other source?" Rod asked remorselessly. He would have done well in my Environmental Studies class. He was likable, intelligent, and he never let go. "You don't think everyone can have a barn covered with solar panels, like you? By the way, can I ask what that cost?"

I almost blushed. Solar cells are still very expensive—about $300 for a panel that will (theoretically) produce 53 watts. Completely installed, my 1.5 kilowatt system cost $18,000.

Rod was hovering. "Too much," I said. And then reluctantly named the figure. Before Rod could pounce, I hurried on. One thing teachers get very good at is talking faster (and louder) than students.

"No, I don't think everybody can have a solar array. Everybody won't have to. When the cost of photovoltaics comes down, as it is bound to when the new roll-roofing-type panels come on the market, power companies can start putting solar energy right into the grid. As a matter of fact, my own little array has an interconnect right now. I feed a few kilowatt-hours into the grid every day the sun shines."

"I hope you're right about cheap solar panels." He did not sound convinced.

"Even if I'm not, you don't have to worry too much about the first half million or so electric cars in California."

"Okay, Prof, why not?"

"Because the California power plants will make that electricity themselves; they have excess nighttime capacity. What's more, they mostly burn natural gas, which puts only a fraction as much stuff in the air as a coal-fired plant. I guess you've heard about Los Angeles Water and Power's offer to EV owners?"

"The discount deal?" Rod said, finishing his second beer. "Two and a half cents off per kilowatt-hour? Yes, I have. I wonder how many people have taken them up on it."

"Well, as it happens, I asked them. Two, at the moment."

"Two!" He barely kept his Wyoming poker face from breaking into a grin.

"I grant you it's not impressive."

"Well," said Rod, "we'll see if they keep it up when there are half a million takers."

We parted friends. I admitted that there are real problems about supplying clean power to large numbers of electric cars. Rod admitted that those problems might be soluble.

The next morning I took a farewell cruise around Laramie. Among other things, being mortally tired of fast food, I found a bakery that also made sandwiches, and got myself a picnic lunch. One way I knew it was a good bakery was that it swarmed with people ordering graduation presents. In Wyoming, you do the same thing at commencement that in Vermont you do for a birthday. You give the kid a cake.

Back at the Laramie Inn, I hitched up. It went more easily than I had feared—took only about ten minutes. First I fastened the tow-bar to the front of the car with two bolts. Then I backed the truck to the exact point where the other end of the bar would fit over the tow-ball, and fastened that. Then I put on the safety chain the law requires, replaced the magnetic signal lights on the car, made sure its gearshift was in neutral (failure to check that was what ruined the MIT car in Victorville in 1968). Finally I cleaned the grease off my hands. At 9:00 A.M. I was ready to go. By noon I was in Nebraska.

CHAPTER 12

Driving after Dark

Does your car turn into a pumpkin if you don't get
home by sunset?
　　—Question from a teenage girl in Kearney,
　　Nebraska.

Now the trip fell into a comfortable pattern. Well, fairly comfortable. Every day I towed Solo two or three hundred miles farther east. Every night I unhitched and took him out alone. I can't claim the days of towing were an actual pleasure. I was still on I-80, still not daring to go faster than fifty or fifty-five, even with my Nevada stones in place, still buffeted by the shock waves from every giant truck that thundered past. Nor can I claim that the evening trips were adventurous. Usually I went no farther than the nearest slow-food restaurant. It was apt to be dark by the time I found a motel and checked in; and while sight-seeing at night works just fine in Reno, if you like that kind of sight, it has a very limited utility going through Nebraska and Iowa.

The mornings were what made this a good time. Going to bed early, I was up early, and I went out again in the electric car. In the brief coolness of a midwestern May morning, I would venture ten or even fifteen miles away from the Great Traffic River. I drove past ranches and stock farms and cornfields; I occasionally trespassed a little. I looked around Kearney, Nebraska—good courthouse here— and Grinnell, Iowa—a simply amazing bank. After the shortest run of the trip, I spent a long time in Iowa City, where there is a splendid university.

I wasn't a bit worried about what to do when Anne arrived, because when I called her from North Platte and told her about the truck's rear plate, she came up with an instant solution. "I'll just take the plates off your farm truck and bring them with me," she said blithely.

"You can't do that," I started to say, but then it struck me that of course, she could. Just not legally. But what possible harm will it do if we use the plates from one Toyota truck on another Toyota truck? Will the truck become any harder to drive? No. Have a longer braking distance? No. Will it be harder for the authorities to identify? No, it will be easier, since the Vermont plates are mine, and those '89 Californias are God knows whose. We're not even cheating any state of revenue, since we can only use one truck at a time. The plates will be sort of like the one tooth and the one eye that the three Fates passed around among themselves in Greek mythology.

I also wasn't worried about whether Anne could get to Peoria on the agreed-on day. She had her ticket. After she taught her two morning classes on Tuesday, May 14, she would drive up to Burlington, Vermont, and catch a plane to Chicago. Then she'd take a little plane to Peoria, where I would be waiting. She'd be able to stay with me until Sunday. By then we expected to be near Cleveland, and I'd put her on a plane back from there.

Airline pricing systems are weird. Why airlines care so much whether you fly home from the same airport you flew out to, I'm not clear. But they do. Her ticket cost so much that she didn't even tell me the figure until I got home, probably for fear I'd have an attack of abstract indignation. For a medium-length flight out and a rather short flight back, she spent $740 of her teacher's salary. It works out to 53 cents a mile.

But I couldn't be indignant, since I didn't know. I was busily and happily playing the tourist. They were placid days between Laramie and Peoria. The only scare I had was in central Nebraska, passing a weigh station for trucks. In Vermont such stations nearly always say "CLOSED," but in the West they seem to stay open more often. This one was not only OPEN, it had a highly ominous sign. All trucks and all pickups with trailers must stop, it said. I definitely was driving a pickup, and a rigorous inspector might argue that Solo constituted a trailer.

Fortunately, the weigh station was not right next to I-80, but a hundred yards or so off to the side, with a little low hill in between. Unless they had an inspector sitting up there with field glasses, it might be possible to slip by. If they zoomed out after me, I wouldn't be in particularly worse trouble than if I turned in, and they happened to notice the expired California plate. Monster trucks, many of them in three sections, obediently turned off; I just kept going, and hoped. No one came out to pursue.

Having got seriously interested in rest areas after my visit with Catherine Logan at Bitter Creek, I stopped at many others as I moved wifewards across Nebraska, Iowa, and Illinois. My favorite was certainly Big Blue River, a little west of Lincoln, Nebraska. Unlike any other I've been in, that one has depth. The actual rest area backs up to the small, not-very-blue, but still pretty river. Then there's a footbridge over the Big Blue (the Little Brown, really), and a path on the other side. If you follow it, you come in a hundred yards or so to a clearing with picnic tables and a piece of sculpture. If you go a little way into the reeds beyond that, you come to an old windmill, such as nearly every farm in Nebraska used to have. It's a metal tower, like a miniature Eiffel, with a round set of blades at the top. This one is rusty and a little bent. But it still works, creaking and croaking as the blades turn. I felt for a second as if I'd stepped into one of Willa Cather's novels—and it's a place I'd like to step. Much as I like Edward Abbey on Utah, I like Willa Cather on Nebraska still better.

Another thing that delighted me in these Midwest rest areas is the way they provide for pets. Provide linguistically, I mean. Each one has a designated "pet exercise area," which is clearly where the dogs are to do their stuff. If you're a human being and you want to do *your* stuff, you seek out the rest rooms in this rest area. If you're an animal, the identical action is called exercising. Wonderful.

More delights. In Iowa, an area that provides for the ancient and traditional act of defecation is called "Modern," while one that doesn't has the label "Undeveloped." At the Krisdala Baka area, near Woodhull, Illinois, there has apparently been trouble with livestock dealers stopping to give their horses and cows a break. At any rate, there is a sign which says firmly, "Large animals are not to be removed from their vehicles for the purpose of grazing, drinking, or exercising." If you've ever seen a cow doing exercises, you will understand the problem.

Krisdala Baka, incidentally, is a new and very handsome place. It is modern in the Iowa sense; one may (unless one is a very large animal) relieve one's bladder there. It is totally old-fashioned in the Wyoming sense. There is neither active nor passive solar, nor did I perceive any energy-saving device of any kind. I saw none in Nebraska, either, and none in Iowa. None—that I passed, anyway—in Pennsylvania or New York. We have one such area in Vermont, and 19 that are not. No big deal: Ohio has 17 that are (and 130 that are not). But only Wyoming seems to be committed to turning them all solar. When this country finally gets around to giving cut-the-pollution prizes, I think Wyoming will get one.

Iowa has generous motels, though. I'm thinking especially of one near Grinnell: the Super-8, surrounded by cornfields, which is run by Liz and Terry Johnson. Stopping for the night, I made the usual request for permission to plug my electric car in.

"Just drive around back, and you can plug it in anywhere you like," Mrs. Johnson said.

"Would three dollars seem fair?"

"Oh, we never charge for that."

"How many electric cars do you get?" I asked, a good deal surprised.

"You're the first. But we get a lot of truckers that like to plug their heaters in, in the winter."

Sure enough, there was a double outlet every twenty feet, all along the back of the motel. The Johnsons won't have to add a thing when electric cars become common. Unless, of course, they want to cover the roof with solar panels, and produce their own virtuous, pollution-free, Rod-approved power.

So far in the trip I had neither seen nor phoned anyone I knew out here in the West and Midwest. There were good reasons. Once I'd abandoned the route AAA designed, which was before I ever left Santa Rosa, I didn't know where I'd be on any given day. In actual fact, where I went was boringly predictable—I had flowed with the Great Traffic River all the way from Vallejo. But that was never a plan. I might easily have turned off and gone adventuring, once I left Nevada. Might have, and rather expected to—heading south into Abbey's country, and then east into Colorado, where I had told a friend in the town of Snowmass I might be dropping by in my electric car. If it hadn't rained so much in Utah, I expect I'd have done it.

Now, in sunny Iowa, I finally made a call. I had just spent a whole morning roaming around Poweshiek County, lured about equally by the rolling farmland and by the town of Grinnell. You might be lured, too, if you came around a corner in a small Iowa town and found a bank with more and better stained glass than the average American cathedral. You might get so curious you'd go in—and then you'd find people doing ordinary bank transactions in a great hall with a fifty-foot ceiling, chandeliers hanging over the tellers' windows, a clock such as might have ornamented the central building in a German principality, and the whole thing designed by Louis Sullivan, inventor of the skyscraper. From the bank, you might get tempted onto the campus of Grinnell College.

So that morning I didn't hook Solo up until it was almost noon, and very hot. And I was hardly back on the river before I started thinking about getting off again. Sixty-five miles ahead lay Iowa City and the University of Iowa. A good friend of mine teaches there. Her name is Kate Hayles. For five years she and I jointly taught a science fiction course to Dartmouth undergraduates. It was while doing that we both came to the disagreeable realization that the human future on this planet is probably going to be blocked by pollution. The third year of that course I also began to teach environmental studies.

There are two rest areas between Grinnell and Iowa City, and I tried to call Kate from both of them. From the second one I got her. It was the end of the school year at the University of Iowa, as it had been at Wyoming. She had a meeting for most of the afternoon, a committee deciding what to do about difficult grades. You know: C-minus and the kid graduates; D-plus, he doesn't.

"Can you stay over?" Kate asked, and of course, I could. While she went to her meeting, I drove on to Iowa City. I parked both vehicles where she'd told me to, prowled around the university in the fierce heat, and finally took refuge in the Zimansky Reading Room. Zimansky has nothing to do with the university library; it's a little private sanctuary for members of the English department, just down the hall from the department offices. This afternoon it was totally empty.

The piece of reading that interested me most was a handwritten notice taped above the coffee machine. It read thus:

> To Coffee Drinkers:
>   Beginning May 8 we will provide
>   the non-biodegradable
>   fluorocarbon-laden styrofoam cups
>   only to guests. Please bring a cup you
>   will keep for yourself.
>   Felicia Lavallee

That's the kind of notice that makes me feel good. Only it seemed mildly puzzling that there were no cups of any sort around, neither styrofoam nor china. Only a lonely jar of Coffee-mate and some white plastic spoons. The spoons had a dusty look. The coffee machine was not on. Today is only May 13th. What can have happened since the eighth to give such a sense of desolation?

Down the hall, in the English office, I found Ms. Lavallee, who is a sort of chief of staff.

I introduced myself as a friend of Professor Hayles. "Can I ask what's happened in Zimansky in the last five days?" I then asked her, and she looked puzzled.

"Nothing, that I know of."

"I mean, since your notice went up on May eighth about the nonbiodegradable, fluorocarbon-laden cups."

Ms. Lavallee started to laugh. "That was two years ago. We've stopped making coffee. The secretaries refused to make it, because they don't drink it themselves, and I fully support them."

That is certainly one way to avoid fluorocarbons.

Kate came in from her meeting, and we did what two teachers would normally do on a sweltering afternoon. We went, not to a cool bar, but to a cool bookstore—the extraordinarily good one called Prairie Lights. Minutes after we got there, Kate introduced me to a bearded young man named Jim, whom I took to be the manager. Then she told him about Solo.

"I've got a friend with an electric car," Jim said. "It's been sitting his garage for ten years now. He bought a conversion kit—he's a good mechanic—and built it himself. He even drove it two or three times. It was totally unreliable."

"Well, mine's not. If it weren't so hot, and if you didn't need to stay in the store, I'd give you a ride right now."

"Let's go," said red-bearded Jim, who is actually the owner.

That night Kate and I went out in the car again, to a restaurant called the Powerhouse. This place *was* a powerhouse once, and outside the whole Iowa River still pours over a six-foot fall. Brown water, running fast. I imagine you could charge a couple of thousand electric cars right here, if they were still generating.

The seven-mile drive to the Powerhouse was nothing, in the warm daylight of a May evening. I felt a touch apprehensive about the drive back, though, because it would be dark and I would be using headlights all the way. It is hard to overcome conditioning. In a gas car, one of the worst things you can do is to leave the lights on with only the battery to feed them. If you drive to work on a misty morning, turn on your so-called parking lights, than forget to turn them off when you actually do park, you are very likely to find a dead battery when you want to go home that evening. As for leaving your actual headlights on, you could probably kill the battery in half an hour.

But in an electric car you *always* have just the battery to feed your lights. This knowledge has made me edgy ever since that first morning of the trip, when I was skirting San Pablo Bay and ignoring the road signs. Yes, I know this car has a big twelve-volt marine battery, not the smaller twelve-volter that gas cars rely on. Yes, I've been using the lights for four straight nights, starting in Laramie. I have had no problems. But until now I haven't asked them to keep shining for more than three or four miles. I would particularly hate to have Solo fail me the very first time I show him off to a friend.

He did not fail. He made the trip back with lights blazing. Out of bravado I even turned the radio on when I saw we were getting pretty close to Kate's house. Her fifteen-year-old son, Jonathan, had gotten home while we were out, and I now offered him a night ride. We went perhaps two miles. So I knew the car was good for at least nine miles after dark, and probably quite a lot more. I also knew one potential flaw in electric cars. Questioned by his mother when we got back, Jonathan said he personally liked the car just fine. But when Kate asked him if it would be a hit at school, he shrugged. "As a novelty, yes. But kids my age, we like noise and we like power. His car is too quiet."

Months later, safely home, I learned that my headlight fears had been wildly exaggerated. There is an organization, called the Battery Council International, which publishes a technical manual on the care and use of storage batteries. I now have a copy. In it I found a table showing which parts of a car use what amounts of electricity. A car radio, for example, draws half an ampere. The interior lights take 2 amps, the parking lights 7, the windshield wipers (at full swing, I assume) 7.5. If you have an air conditioner in the car, that takes 24. And what about headlights? What do they need? Low beams take only 9, hardly more than parking lights. I worried too much.

CHAPTER 13

The Car on Its Own Again

The real tourist—the one who gets the most enjoyment
and education from the sport—is he who is satisfied to
make from 60 to 80 miles a day, to travel slowly, speed-
ing only on the level, deserted roads. . . .
    —C. H. GILLETTE in *The Horseless Age,* June 24,
      1903

THE NEXT MORNING at 7:30, I drove silently into the university parking lot where my truck had spent the night, and hitched up. This is a pay lot—unless you're a university employee, and have a key—and I should have paid five dollars. Maybe more, if you want to consider that I had two vehicles. But the college-age boy on the gate had been watching from his booth. "Today is free for electric cars," he said cheerily, and waved me through. Soon I was sailing back onto the Great Traffic River.

Just beyond Bettendorf, Iowa, I crossed the real great river, the Mississippi; and then, a few miles into Illinois, I finally left I-80 and headed south for Peoria. The Regional Airport is easy to find, and of a totally nonthreatening size. I was there by early afternoon. But unlike any other airport I've ever been to (except Post Mills, Vermont, which mostly serves hot-air balloons), it is not surrounded by motels. An hour's driving around gave me a growing familiarity with the towns of Bellevue and West Peoria, but no clue to a place where Anne and I and the two vehicles could spend the night. Then, in the village of Bartonville, south of the airport, the same serendipity that had caused me to meet Paul, the young refrigeration expert in Davis, California, and to run into John Fratcher in Auburn now put me in the path of a slim, goateed man whose name I never learned.

"I take it that's your electric car outside," he began, having tracked me into the empty fast-foodery where I was drinking about a quart of water, along with a small Coke. "Mind if I join you? I'm about to build one, and I'd like to take a look at yours."

I am always glad to leave a Hardee's, and out we went. In five minutes he knew the car better than I do. He asked me why it didn't have regenerative braking, and then answered the question himself. "I see, you've just one motor."

"How many should it have?" I asked, surprised.

"Two. One for each drive wheel, and then you don't need a transmission."

"Oh."

Now he was peering at my one motor, which is half-hidden under a row of batteries. "How many horsepower?"

That I could answer. "Twenty-three."

He nodded. "Yes, that's about average."

Was I talking to some senior engineer at the local power company? I was not. Though we never traded names, the slender man and I talked a long time, and I learned something of his life. He started as a plumber, later switched to repairing clocks and watches. He did not say this in so many words—he was not a boastful man—but I was clear he felt confident of his ability to put just about anything together, including an EV. It is one of the best things I know about the United States that it contains people like Paul McNeal and John Fratcher and this man. They don't have, and don't need, degrees or Dartmouths or any formal accreditation at all. They see something worth doing, and do it. There may also be some natural affinity between clock-and-watch people and electric cars. As I learned after I got home from the trip, the Swiss firm that makes Swatches is about to go full tilt into the EV business.

Before we parted, I asked the man about motels. He considered a minute. "Well, there really aren't any near the airport. But if you cross the river, you'll find some older ones." He thought a minute more, and gave me directions to one in the town of Creve Coeur.

The name delighted me. Hector St. John de Crèvecoeur, for whom it obviously was named, has been a presence in my life. He was a French army lieutenant in Canada, who left military service in 1759 to become a farmer in upstate New York. The book he wrote about that experience—*Letters from an American Farmer*—was the first best seller ever written in this country. It was also one of the first books that Alison and her classmates had to read when they took Environmental Studies 1 with me. There's even a town near my wife's farm in Vermont called St. Johnsbury, and that, too, is named for de Crèvecoeur. We often shop there.

So I happily drove across the Illinois River, into Creve Coeur, and found the Ragon Motel right where the slender man said it would be. It is a sort of Midwest counterpart of the Ranch Motel in Citrus Heights. Once it must have been a fancy place: brick units facing each other across a wide cement court. There was still a notice pasted to the mirror in the unit I rented for Anne and me: "Switchboard closes 11:30 P.M. After hours kindly use pay phone at front of motel." That must go back to before dial telephones.

Anne's plane got in about 8:00 P.M. and we drove back across the Illinois, which is a big river, headlights on high beam, 13 amps. Soon we were two of the roughly six people spending the night at the tattered Ragon Motel.

There was no hitching up to do in the morning, merely a little quick fiddling with the license plates. Anne had the Vermont ones with her—they hadn't even made anything buzz at the airport—and they attached easily. Then we were off. Not even pausing for breakfast, we started along Illinois 24 in a caravan of two. I went ahead in Solo. Anne followed in the truck. Nothing symbolic, just prudence. "That way I can keep an eye on you," she had said. "It won't be *me* that has to stop first."

It surely wouldn't be. Even pulling the car, that little truck had on occasion gone 280 miles without stopping. Solo's current record was 33 miles. It's not that the California truck was any less a guzzler than the one back in Vermont whose license plates it now bore; it probably guzzled more. But it had a gas tank you could practically go swimming in. Fill it up, and you pumped 19 gallons.

Naturally I hope to improve Solo's record today. With Anne behind me in the follow-truck, I wouldn't get panicked on yellow and red bar, as I had on Business 101 and in Meadow Vista. I'd just keep going until I actually ran out of power. I was hoping that wouldn't happen for fifty miles.

But setting a new distance record for the car was not our only plan for the day. We also had touristy thoughts. Neither of us had ever driven across the Midwest. Both of us love handsome buildings. Anne had gotten a little jealous of my glowing accounts of the courthouse in Kearney, and that incredible bank in Grinnell, and also of what I had seen more recently—just yesterday, in fact—the great turreted, square-towered, Norman-arched courthouse in Galesburg, Illinois.

You do not, at present, see many beautiful buildings in American cities. Most of them have been torn down, because the site was wanted for something else. The new replacement is never beautiful? Of course. Occasionally it's even stunning. But more frequently a beautiful old building is replaced by a commonplace new one—or in the case of skyscrapers and such, thirty or forty beautiful old buildings are replaced by one mediocre new one.

For good-looking buildings that still exist, it's better to go to mere towns. Towns grow more slowly (otherwise they'd have become cities), and thus have less frequent opportunity to cannibalize themselves.

But you still have an ordeal to face. To see the good-looking part of a town in California, you have to get through the elephantiasis zone. In most other parts of the country, it's an eczema ring you have to get through. Some say scrofula. The scale is not vast, as in California, but the principle is the same. Where the outskirts of an American town used to be, the sidewalks vanishing, the houses getting farther apart, the first farm or two appearing, now there are K Marts and Wal-Marts and motels and Tastee-Freezes and Hardee's. Nobody walks to these places; it is all but forbidden. You drive in from the country, or out from town. And because you are therefore looking for your destination from a moving vehicle, all these new constructs have giant signs that you will notice at 35 mph. A way to make giant signs beautiful has yet to be invented.

When a town is quite small, though, it often doesn't have an eczema ring. There just aren't enough people around to make it worthwhile. We have a good many uninfected towns in Vermont. It was in hopes of more that Anne and I were driving along Illinois 24. Gridley, 1,800 people; Chatsworth, 1,200; Chenoa, 1,850. It sounded promising.

But the first town we came to after Creve Coeur (which I am afraid is mainly eczema) was a bigger place. Eureka, the seat of Woodford County, is a town of 4,000.

Eureka has only the lightest rash of shopping centers. What it has, besides a good place to get breakfast, is a fine Renaissance courthouse, built of light tan stone. "I want to see it," Anne said instantly, and in we went. We stayed so long, admiring the rotunda, that a woman in uniform noticed us, and came over. The result of *that* was that we soon found ourselves in court. Not because we were in trouble, but because Deputy Sheriff Betty McCanless was proud of her courthouse and proud of the judges, and she wanted us to see one of them in action. We got the newer, younger one, Judge Mark Dalton, at a sentencing hearing. And we got him in person afterwards. Deputy McCanless liked her judge (she's right to) and she liked us, so when the hearing was over, she brought him down from the bench. The judge liked the idea of our electric car trip.

El Paso, Texas, is a city of half a million. El Paso, Illinois, far less well known, is a town of 2,500, ten miles past Eureka. It has a hint of fallen grandeur. The City Opera House, another Renaissance building, still stands, is in good repair, gets used. It's wonderfully handsome, with its round tower growing out of the facade, as if someone had planted a tower seed about 100 years ago, and with its fresh white paint over brick and stone. But it is too near the derelict railroad station. And much as I love cows, it does seem a comedown for it to be housing the Illinois Dairy Association.

Gridley, Chenoa, Fairbury, Chatsworth: It was a nice road. For a long time Solo rolled along by himself. He was going east under his own power for the first time since we had to turn back at Meadow Vista. There was no turning back today. He went thirty-five miles, then forty, then forty-five, and still the fuel gauge stayed on green bar. Finally at fifty-one it flashed to yellow. I kept going; Anne was right behind. At fifty-seven the gauge turned to red. I still kept going. But now Solo's power was perceptibly slackening, and at fifty-eight I pulled over. If we had wanted to wait fifteen or twenty minutes, the batteries would have repolarized enough for me to reach at least sixty. But it was a hot afternoon, as hot as Iowa City, and we preferred to hitch up and keep going.

The place where we hitched was getting on toward the state line, and we spent that night in Monticello, Indiana. This is in a region of lakes, all of which have eczema along their shores. I got a good charge at the Lake Terrace Motel, though, and on the morning of May 16 we again set out in caravan. The little city of Logansport did not tempt us, though Cass County's nearby park and waterfall did. "Could you still drive that car if it was a cloudy day?" asked the green-uniformed ranger when we turned in.

Late that morning we got to Peru, another of the eleven county seats strung along Highway 24. Behind me in the truck, Anne gave a triple beep, her signal to stop.

"I want to see this one, too," she said, pointing to the ballustraded, Doric-columned, Ionic-columned, high-rotunda'd courthouse in the center of town. We spent no time in court here, though I did fall into a visit with Nancy Hardwick, the county assessor—and wound up wishing Vermont assessed farmland the way Indiana does.

A little past Wabash, at fifty-three miles, green turned to yellow. At fifty-eight, yellow turned to red. I pulled over instantly, and though we were in a land without shadows and the heat was fierce, we waited fifteen minutes to see what the batteries would do. With that much rest, what they would do was take us to sixty-two miles before I felt the power begin to fade. Not bad. All that was ever promised by Solar Electric. Of course, it took the perfectly level terrain of Illinois and Indiana to produce it. No wonder that in the year 1900 Buffalo, New York, had more electric cars than any other American city its size. Buffalo was on flatter ground than any other American city its size. Presumably still is. If I can run this car satisfactorily in Vermont, where you get down one hill only to start at once up another, it will mean that anyone can run an electric. Well, except people who live partway up Donner Pass, and those Swiss who inhabit Alpine villages. Or, considering Swatch's plans, maybe they can, too.

Soon after hitching up, we left Indiana 24, and swung north. This was partly because we would otherwise have been carried into Fort Wayne, and partly because a lawyer in Wabash had told us about the courthouse in Columbia City. "It's nothing special inside," he said. "What you're going to like is the dome."

He was right. We began to like it while we were still several miles south of this city of 5,000. It seems to hover above the trees in a way that I had hitherto thought was special to northern Italy. It was a good place to spend the night, and to learn a little about vice presidents. Not just Quayle, who comes from the next county seat south of here, but another and greater one, Thomas Riley Marshall, a lawyer of Columbia City, and Woodrow Wilson's vice president for eight years. It might be a different world had he taken over the presidency, as most scholars agree he should have, after Wilson's stroke in 1919. President Wilson, incidentally, sometimes drove exactly the way I was driving now. He owned a Baker electric. The Secret Service did not have any EVs. So he'd go out for a drive, followed by a Secret Service agent in a Cadillac, like Anne in the Toyota.

We visited two more courthouses the next day. One was in the tiny town of Albion, the seat of Noble County. There the sight of an electric car parked on the courthouse square produced a fast enough reaction so that we were still on the second floor of the courthouse, admiring a group of fresco portraits, when the second media event of the trip occurred. It was a lot more fun than the first. A woman came rapidly up the steps.

"Are you the folks with the electric car?" she asked?

"We are."

"Would you mind being interviewed?"

"Not a bit."

"Oh, good. I'm Joy LeCount, editor of the *Albion New Era*. First, let me ask how you happen to be in Albion in an electric car with Vermont plates."

I told her. She asked a dozen other questions. Then Anne said,

"Now we have a question for you. It's about this portrait."

There were four fresco portraits on the second floor of the court-house, old ones. Like all proper frescoes, they were unlabeled. Two we had easily identified as Washington and Lincoln. The third we were pretty sure was Andrew Jackson. The fourth had us stumped.

Joy looked at it a minute, consulted a legal-looking woman coming down the hall with some papers, and then led us to a framed letter hanging on the courthouse wall. There is some dissension, said the letter, about how Noble County comes to be Noble County. Because a man named Noah Noble happened to be governor of Indiana at the time the county came into being, everybody thought it was named for him. They were wrong. What they were forgetting was that Noah Noble had a brother named James, who happened to be the first U.S. senator Indiana ever sent to Washington—and it's mostly for him that Indiana towns like Noblesville (Hamilton County) and Noble (Jay County) are named. We liked his picture. It was a sad blow when we learned from Joy much later that the fourth portrait is actually of President McKinley.

Our last courthouse was in Auburn, Indiana, and it was a very grand one. We didn't give it as much time as it deserved, though, because I got so excited when a lawyer we were talking to mentioned that there was an antique car museum in town. Why would there be one of these in an Indiana town of under ten thousand? Easy. Auburn was once a small Detroit. They made Auburns and Cords and Due-senbergs, and all three were the sorts of cars that Jay Gatsby would have loved to drive.

Neither Anne nor I had ever been in a car museum, nor felt any urge to go—but then, we had never owned an electric car before. We wasted no time getting to this museum. There were 140 old cars on display. Most of them, obviously, were Cords, Duesenbergs, and Au-burns. One, however, was an 1899 Waverley Stanhope phaeton, an electric car made in Indianapolis. And one was a 1916 Rauch & Lang coach, an electric car made in Cleveland. They were the first early EVs I had ever seen.

To compare the two was fascinating. The 1899 Waverley looked truly primitive. Electric cars were not brand-new in 1899—on the contrary, one had appeared on a Broadway stage in 1897, when the

Electrical transport during the early days, from top to bottom, then left to right: the Waverley 1903 Electric Surrey, made in Indianapolis; the Baker Electric of 1899—"The first electric vehicle driven on the streets of Cleveland"; the Baker Electric "Newport Model" of 1900; the Lohner-Porsche Electric Coupe of 1903.

stage manager of the Metropolitan Opera and some friends put on a burlesque version of Gounod's *Faust*. In their version, Faust tries to elope with Marguerite in an electric taxicab. Even earlier, in 1895, there had been an electric car onstage in London, for a Christmas pantomime. Cinderella went to the ball in it.

All the same, the 1899 Waverley was truly primitive. It looked exactly as if you had taken a buggy away from some horse, put bicycle tires on it, and then installed a tiller to steer with. It had no instruments or gauges of any kind. Not one. According to a label the museum had attached, the Waverley could go 12 to 14 miles an hour, and had a range of 40 miles. (My car would have a range of 100 miles at that speed—I just don't care to drive 12 or 14 mph.) In short, it could do about what a horse could, with the difference that it didn't need to be caught in the pasture, or harnessed.

The Rauch & Lang five-passenger coach was strikingly different. Where you were open to the weather in the old Waverley, here you had glass all around—more glass than in a contemporary car. A *lot* more glass than in early gasoline cars. Ninety-nine percent of them had none, except maybe a windshield. They were open vehicles. I think the manufacturers felt uneasy about the exhaust fumes, and didn't want to risk asphyxiating new owners. But electric vehicles of every sort could and did button right up. Consider that forgotten milestone of ambulance history: the delivery, in February 1900, of the first electric ambulance in the United States. It belonged to St. Vincent's Hospital in New York. This behemoth weighed 4,000 pounds, and could go only nine miles an hour. But no one caught pneumonia on the way to St. Vincent's. "By means of plate glass windows in the front and sides and glass doors at the rear, the vehicle can be entirely enclosed."

While I'm at it, I might mention that EVs were also first with power steering. There was a ten-ton electric truck in Paris that had it in 1901—and the editor of the first automobile magazine in America wrote in an admiring editorial that he believed it to be the only vehicle in the world thus equipped. But it wasn't. There were electric taxis with power steering cruising around Paris in 1897.

Unlike the little Waverley, the 1916 Rauch & Lang was loaded with instruments. It had a voltmeter, a running ammeter like John Fratcher's, a fuel gauge that showed the charge in ampere-hours, and a speedometer. Unlike any other car I have ever seen (except another Rauch & Lang, later) it also had provision for a backseat driver. In fact, you *had* to drive from the back seat, because that's where the tiller was. I presume a chauffeur usually sat back there, while the owners were in front and got the view. What it didn't have was the ability to keep up with gas cars. Top speed: twenty-five.

A little beyond Auburn, we got back on an interstate, and though Solo had done only fifty-one miles on his own power and was still on yellow, it seemed like a good time to hitch up again. Before dusk we were in Fremont, Ohio, checking in to a motel. Like a surprising number of Midwest motels, this one was managed by an Indian. I don't mean a Native American, but a person whose ancestors came from India. The man here was delighted to let us plug in for an extra three dollars, and happy to spend an hour or so figuring out the most complicated way to do it.

"I won't give you a room until I see what will work best," he said.

His first thought was an outlet at the base of the motel's neon sign. When we tried it, he saw that either my orange cord would go across a corner of the paved parking area or else Solo would have to roll up on the grass near the sign. Neither was acceptable.

Then he considered having me park in front of the row of units, as people usually do at motels. But that would mean running the cord across the narrow walkway that went the length of the motel. Also unacceptable, even though no guest ever seemed to use the walkway. They went straight out from their doors to their cars, six feet away. If they wanted to go to the office, they drove.

Finally the manager decided to give us No. 10, because it had both an electric outlet on its front wall and a piece of iron grillwork that supported a gutter. Here the cord could go straight from Solo's plug up the grille, over the walkway at a height of seven feet, and then down the front wall of the unit to the outlet. Sort of like a grapevine in a grape arbor.

"I will thread your cord through the grille, carry it over, and then tape it to the wall," the manager said. He went off to the office, and came back with a roll of remarkable flimsy tape. It didn't, of course, hold the heavy orange cord. Not even when he had put on twelve strips.

"I will have to get a nail from my house," he announced; and, springing into his car, he drove about 200 yards to where he lived. All this being provisional, we still did not have access to No. 10. By now I was longing for the wild free days on Business 101, when I could just fling one end of the cord out my second-story window, and down to Solo.

Fortunately, the front wall of the motel was composed of boards (rather than, say, cement blocks); and after a short delay while he fetched a stepladder (I supplied the hammer), the manager was able to drive the nail in, attach the cord to it, and finally award us the key to No. 10. We left Solo charging, and went off to a fish dinner in Port Clinton.

Some instinct made me check the car when we got back, and the instinct was sound. It was no longer charging. Could the manager have turned the circuit off the minute we left? Doubtful. Did we consider notifying him? Not on your life. There was a Coke machine no more than six feet down the walk toward No. 9, and an unoccupied half of a double outlet beside it. I shifted the cord to that. No friendly hum of charging batteries resulted. Perhaps Solo had tripped a breaker.

Anne rises to these occasions. She now took the light bulb out of the flimsy lamp outside our door, and started to screw the adapter in, the same one I'd used in Citrus Heights. It didn't fit. So, passing a lot more cord up the grille, overhead, and down past the nail, she brought the end in through the door, and plugged into a reading lamp. I was careful to set the charger on Low.

Why Solo had almost no charge the next morning, I have never figured out. I don't see what the manager could possibly have done. The other reading lamp still worked. But the gauge had risen only from low yellow bar to high yellow bar, and that the batteries could easily do by themselves. Did we consider asking for our three dollars back? We hitched up as fast as possible, and set off for Cleveland.

CHAPTER 14

Cleveland

By reason of their refined appearance, comfort, elegance, and simplicity of operation, they [EVs] are admirably adapted to ladies' own use.
—M. J. BUDLONG, "The Development of the
Electric Automobile," *Harper's Weekly,* March
17, 1907

IF I WAS TERRIFIED of Chicago, how could I now be deliberately aiming for Cleveland? And not just to drop a passenger at the airport, but to drive into the middle of the city and spend the night there. Well, first, it helps to have a cool and resourceful wife along. Anne can read a street sign at fifty yards. She can smell a traffic jam two blocks away. She can even back up a truck that has an electric car attached behind. Even, or perhaps especially, if it says on the tow-bar not to do this. Venturing alone into Chicago and cruising companionably into Cleveland are very different things.

But secondly, we had a clear destination, and directions to it. Old friends of mine live in Cleveland, and the day after Anne got her ticket, I called them. It turned out they'd be away when we arrived, but could put us up anyway—not in their empty house, but, rather grandly, downtown. Wendell teaches at Case Western Reserve. The university owns a mansion that once belonged to a paint millionaire, and uses it to put up guests. Wendell wangled us a reservation for Saturday night. It was Saturday morning when we hurried out of

Fremont. Tonight we'd be at the mansion; tomorrow Anne flew home.

One good thing about chemistry professors, which Wendell is, is that they give excellent directions. We got easily into the center of Cleveland, and we easily went up the right one-way street for Glidden House. Checking in was a little harder. The parking at the mansion was not designed with trailer-trucks in mind, not even miniature ones. It had not even been designed for as many cars as were present. So we unhitched in the street, and each waited in a vehicle until someone pulled out of a spot, then moved like lightning. In twenty minutes we were both parked, and we could go in and register. Glidden House is a true plutocratic mansion: stately rooms, deep carpets, conservatory, a library full of books. Boccherini playing instead of Muzak. This was going to be a nifty change from motels. I just hoped that being so grand, they wouldn't get stuffy about poor Solo.

I therefore didn't even mention the car until the clerk had handed us our room key. Then I began my pitch. "We're driving an electric car," I said—and at that point the clerk politely broke in.

"Professor Williams told us about your car. You are quite welcome to charge it outside."

Permission is not enough, of course. I also needed an outlet. I walked entirely around the mansion without spotting one. Then I walked around again. Perhaps we'd need to use a window, after all? Fortunately, at that moment I noticed the pergola on the side lawn. I slipped over and checked that. Two outlets, near the ground. It would be a long reach from Solo's parking place—but fasten them together and my two orange cords will go a hundred feet. I made the connection with a yard to spare.

Glidden House has a wonderful location. In one direction we could walk over to Severance Hall, where the Cleveland Symphony plays, and get tickets for tonight. In the other, we could walk maybe a quarter of a mile and come to another car museum. This one had 200 cars, 5 of them electrics. I spent much of Saturday afternoon looking at them.

The most interesting was a 1904 Baker. Put it, in one's mind, next to the 1899 Waverley, and it showed clearly what the early stages of

EV development were. Look at it just in itself, and you saw what caused the enormous early popularity of electric cars.

The horse influence was still strong in 1904. If the Waverley looked like a buggy with bicycle tires, the Baker looked like a surrey with a headlight. It even had a fringe on top. Any horse would have recognized it as a close cousin of things it had pulled. The horse would, of course, have been deeply suspicious of that big round electric headlight, mounted, like a locomotive's, in the middle. And if it poked its head into the driver's seat (as a horse really did to a parked EV in Indianapolis in the winter of 1901, accidentally starting it, and causing a medium-serious accident), it would have found other disturbing things: a voltmeter, an ammeter, several kinds of levers.

But more interesting than any of the controls was a piece of paper in a frame, next to the car. Some curator at the Western Reserve Historical Society had found a full-page magazine ad for 1904 Bakers, and there it was, neatly framed. Whoever wrote the ad was not strong on grammar—but he was very clear who he hoped to sell Bakers to. About the 1904 model he wrote this: "Being absolutely free of lubricants, the finest gowns may be worn by its occupants." Mrs. Woodrow Wilson, for example.

In general, early motorcars were an exclusively male thing. Men owned them, men did all the driving. (Even in my youth, "woman driver" was still a term of reproach.) Men also turned the cranks that started them, and got greasy up to the elbows doing the daily maintenance. Of course, there were early women drivers, perhaps the most famous being the great English racing driver Dorothy Levitt. Such women expected to get dirty. When Ms. Levitt wrote a book called *The Woman and the Car,* in 1909, one of her earliest pieces of advice was to forget the fine gowns. Leave them home. "Indispensible to the motoriste who is going to drive her own car is the overall. . . . Remember, it is better to get grease-spots on your washable overall than on your coat or other clothes."

Ms. Levitt also suggested a few things that the woman driver might want to keep in her car. In addition, that is, to her tire repair kit and perhaps a small revolver. The list reads thus: "Ammeter, jack, pliers, spanners, carburettor jet key, large and small screw-drivers,

hammer, oil can, grease-injector, tyre-pump, sparking-plug, inlet
and exhaust valves, trembler blade and screw, some washers, split
pins, file, very fine file for platinum points, emery-powder, insulated
tape, and some waste or swabs."

A similar list for an early electric car would certainly have included the tire repair kit—though even there, since early EVs were
used mainly in cities, some manufacturers offered a solid-tire model
which never got flats. Beyond that, what? Well, here's what Tom
Swift, the boy inventor, took along in his electric runabout in 1910.
He was on his way to a big race. Into the car he packed "spare fuses,
extra parts, wires, and different things he thought he might need."
Those "different things" probably included pliers, wrenches, and a
couple of screwdrivers, but nothing like Ms. Levitt's list. An electric
motor simply has fewer parts, needs no lubricants, produces no
waste. It is clean.

For this reason, as well as for the car's ease of starting, electrics
were the only cars that most women cared to drive a century ago. In
Chicago in the fall of 1900, for example, there were eight women
with driver's licenses. All eight were licensed on electrics, and no
women were licensed on gasoline cars. The chief city engineer, who
sat on the licensing board, estimated that there were actually about
fifty women driving in Chicago—forty-two of them just didn't have
licenses. They were EV drivers to a woman.

Ease of starting is no longer exclusive to EVs. Cleanness still is.
It's a different kind of cleanness, of course, and even more important
than the 1910 variety. It's a nice thing not to get grease spots on
one's gown, or on one's jeans, either. But it is vital not to make holes
in one's planet's ozone layer.

From the car museum we walked to the Cleveland Museum of
Art—whose cafeteria, incidentally, contains a lesson. The lesson is
that you don't have to go to fast-food chains for quick service, and
you don't have to go to grand restaurants for quality. That cafeteria
offers both. I liked the instantly served, perfectly seasoned mush-
room soup so much that I had hardly eaten the last spoonful before I
found myself getting up to go back for another bowl. While I was
there, I got Anne and me each another of the Paris-quality hard

French rolls. At twenty-seven cents apiece, these strike me as one of the best food bargains in the United States.

From the art museum we walked to Euclid Avenue, and then we walked to Severance Hall to hear Mahler, and finally we walked back to the guest mansion. Just before bed I walked out to the parking lot. Last night's fiasco in Fremont was much on my mind. It seemed only common sense to step out and make sure that nothing had disturbed that long cord. Nothing had. Solo was charging nicely. I did get a small surprise when I went to the pergola, though. Someone was in it. He stood up when I arrived. "Hi," he said. "I was just having me a little rest." A street person, he sounded like, but not an ominous one.

"Hi," I answered. "I'm just checking my car."

I must not have sounded ominous to him, either, because he started to chat. "You always have to plug that car in?" he asked curiously.

"If I want to drive it, I do."

"It run just on electricity?"

"Yes, and a little bit of that the car makes itself."

"How it do that?"

"Come on over, and I'll show you."

He studied Solo's panels for a minute, asked about rainy days, asked about the range. Then he pulled out a pack of cigarettes, took one himself, offered me one. "I like that," he said approvingly. "Savin' energy."

On Sunday morning, Solo was fully charged. When I had eaten all the Glidden House croissants I could possibly hold, Anne and I went for what in 1904 they would have called a spin. We took Solo down to Lake Erie. Soon we drove into Gordon State Park, right on the lake, to take one more walk. It was here that my tentative theory about Midwest modesty crumbled. I had begun to form it in Iowa, noting those euphemistic "pet exercise areas," those coyly "modern" rest areas. But here the dominant note, as you entered the park, was a four-foot by eight-foot sign, painted red, white, and green. GORDON PARK LATRINE BUILDING, it said in large letters, and under that "Your Tax Dollars at Work for a Better Ohio." Under that, "Dept. of Natural

Resources, State of Ohio." Human urine certainly is a natural resource, though not of much use if you merely centralize it in a latrine building. All that urea and hippuric acid would make a great fertilizer for the center strips of interstates.

We took a leisurely walk along the shore. There were a good many fishermen pulling catches out of a lake that twenty years ago some of the more excitable environmentalists were ready to call dead. Were ready to, and did. Environmentalists have a special obligation, I think, not to play Chicken Little unless they can say with a high degree of probability that the sky really is about to fall. An environmentalist who exaggerates may do almost as much harm as the government or corporate official who denies that there's a problem at all.

By noon it was time to hitch up, take Anne to the airport, and resume the eastward journey. Solo would once again have to tag along, like the riding horse or family cow tied to the back of the pioneer family's covered wagon.

CHAPTER 15

Little Electric and Big Electric

This car climbed Mt. Washington.
  —Bumper sticker on an electric car in Rotterdam,
  New York

IT IS NOT FAR from Cleveland to the Pennsylvania border, and no distance at all across the little strip of Pennsylvania that comes up to touch Lake Erie. By late afternoon I was in New York, on its Thruway. I don't even like the spelling.

I got off at the first exit, Mayville-Chautauqua. From here I had only to drive three or four hundred miles across New York State, duck into Vermont at Fair Haven, cross the Green Mountains, and I'd be home. I saw no reason to do this last bit of the journey on a big road. Especially not one like the Thruway that bristles with toll-booths. I had already put out seventy cents to go from the border to the first exit: thirty-five cents for the pickup, and thirty-five cents more for Solo.

Mayville is the kind of small town that has white houses and wide lawns. It also seemed to be entirely free of eczema, and partly for that reason it felt eastern to me. A narrow country road led on down toward Jamestown, following the western shore of Lake Chautauqua. I took it, and in a few miles I came to something called the Southern Tier Expressway: two lanes in each direction, and almost devoid of traffic. It headed due east, first crossing the lake on a bridge. Completely forgetting my resolution about big roads, I got right on.

An hour later I got off again, but only because it was growing dark, and I had been driving for many miles through an enormous forest. When I saw a sign for the town of Salamanca, it seemed like a good idea to stop. It was. To begin with, Salamanca has an actual hotel, left from its railroad days. Now it's called the Dudley Motor Inn, but that's mere adaptation. It's a four-story *hotel*, with a good dining room. After the guest mansion and the Boccherini, I was a little reluctant to drop back immediately to motels, and now I didn't have to.

Salamanca also has an electric car enthusiast, a sandy-haired man named Richard Wojcik. He came over before I had even parked (there is room behind the Dudley for almost anything), and began asking questions at a faster clip than anybody since the college boy in Auburn, California. "If you're going to be around a few days," he suggested presently, "maybe you could give a talk in the high school, educate a few people."

"I'm leaving tomorrow. But I'll give you a ride before I go, if you like."

"What time?"

We settled on eight o'clock.

Best of all, in Salamanca I encountered another EV, the second one of the trip. Second one outside a museum, anyway. Richard and I had taken our ride. I'd visited the Seneca Iroquois National Museum, and heard from one of its curators a good deal of the early history of Salamanca, back when it was called Hemlock, and there were no railroads, and the Iroquois owned the whole valley, as technically they still do. Now I was behind the hotel, trying to hitch up. The tow-bar refused to go on. I was afraid I knew why. In the last few days Anne and I had both gotten rather good at backing up. Once she had gone back almost twenty feet, when our way forward got blocked in a parking lot in Watseka, Illinois. I had done a shorter but still daring backup only yesterday, at the Cleveland airport. That and two or three other retrograde movements were presumably what had bent the bar enough so that it was now proving impossible to fit its front end over the tow-ball.

While I was whacking away with a hammer, a tall, gray-haired man appeared. "You need some help, I guess," he said.

"I'd love it."

The tall man had me reposition the two vehicles, and when he judged I had them right, he tricked the bar by suddenly jumping on it full force. It went over the tow-ball with a thunk. Good maneuver—but is it one I can repeat, working alone? Doubtful. Maybe I'll just leave Solo hitched until I get home. It's only a couple of days.

The man stayed to talk. Pretty soon I knew his name was Jack O'Brien, that he was in the cleaning business, that he had two young grandchildren named Tracy and Jay. Then he remarked casually that he kept an electric car for them to drive when they came to visit, and would I like to see it? Would a Muslim like to see Mecca? Would Gutenberg like to see a Bible?

"Yes, please," I said. We walked the 100 yards over to his cleaning establishment, where he kept the car between visits.

I knew perfectly well he meant a toy car, but since it ran on batteries and transported human beings, I was still dying to see it. It turned out to be a blue plastic EV, weighing about forty pounds. I could pick it up, and did. But it was genuine for all that. A one-seater. You weren't supposed to drive if you were under three, Jack said, and by the time you were seven you could no longer fit in. But any child between those ages could hop in and drive around the parking lot behind the Dudley Motor Inn either in Low at 2 ½ mph or in High at 5 mph. He or she could keep driving all day long.

"Except when he or she needs a new charge," I said.

"Oh, no. I charge it up the night before the kids come. Then they can use it all day on that one charge."

When Jack said that, a memory stirred in my mind. I thought of the Cuban midget. A year earlier, reading old car magazines, I'd seen a brief account of what was said to be the world's smallest electric car, owned by one of the world's smallest women. The author made an outrageous claim about how long this car would go between charges.

After I got home, I looked the article up. It ran in *The Horseless Age* for June 26, 1901. The tiny woman was named Chiquita, and she was two feet two inches tall. The article didn't give her last name. Her tiny car was three feet long. The Jenkins Automobile Company of Washington, D.C., had built it for her: "a little electric Victoria, complete with top, electric lights and gong, fenders, and steering wheel gear." It was designed for Chiquita to use on city streets as well as on stages—and that's not as absurd as you may think. If mopeds can mingle in traffic, why not three-foot motorcars? There's no actual virtue in lugging a ton of steel around, every time someone drives to the store for a quart of milk.

But now came the incredible part. The company claimed that Chiquita's car would "run for 2,000 hours with absolutely no attention except that required to control and guide it."

I didn't believe that then, and I don't believe it now. Two thousand hours comes to 83 days. Chiquita could drive continuously for 83 days, without even any help from solar panels, which hadn't been invented yet? Impossible. The company must really have meant she could count on 2,000 hours with no repairs or maintenance. That's still pretty good. It's about 1,990 more maintenance-free hours than any gasoline-car manufacturer would have dared to claim in 1901. It's 1,000 or so more, I think, than any would claim right now.

Anyway, the more I thought about Tracy and Jay and their blue plastic car, the more it struck me that Chiquita probably *could* go an exceptionally long time between charges. It's the light weight that makes the difference.

Put a substantial grandchild—say, a kid weighing 60 pounds—in the blue plastic EV, and you still have only 100 pounds total weight. As for Chiquita, a woman a full foot shorter than the average six-year-old, she and her car might weigh in at 80 pounds. Solo weighs a good bit more. So do I.

I can't and don't want to shrink, but the car is another matter. If you could cut the weight in half, you would simultaneously double the range. Maybe even triple it. Solo, as I learned after I got him home and was able to put him on the scales at the feed store in St. Johnsbury, weighs 3,300 pounds. Twenty-one hundred pounds of that is car, and 1,200 is batteries. What if you had a 1,050-pound car, still with 1,200 pounds of batteries? I think you might go over Donner Pass with some ease. I dearly love Solo. But my next electric car is going to be lighter.

From Salamanca I rambled along the Southern Tier Expressway, making frequent side excursions. One of these was to the county seat of Allegany County, a small town called Belmont. I wanted to see how an upstate New York courthouse compared to those glorious buildings in Illinois and Indiana. It was no contest. Belmont has a perfectly ordinary neocolonial brick courthouse, dating from 1937. And a somewhat less than ordinary annex, made of cement blocks. Only the cornerstone of what I would have wanted to see—the old 1859 courthouse—was still there.

In every other way, though, Belmont delighted me. Like Mayville, it has no rash of fast-food places on the outskirts: just farms and a gravel company. Pass them, and abruptly you're in the little town. Like Salamanca, it has kept its hotel. Belmont House is slightly run-down inside, but the brick and stone exterior is breathtaking. Like Laramie, Wyoming, it's full of people with the environment on their minds. In an hour I met or heard about three. Tom Barber, a technician for Blaktop, has a solar hot-water tank and plans for a full solar house as soon as he and his wife can sell their present one. Fred Rassman has a full solar house already. Ron Lundberg, a retired science teacher, and his wife, Gloria, have both solar panels and a wind generator.

There's a persistent myth that solar technology pays off only in dry, sunny places well to the south, such as Phoenix, Arizona. People who believe that might want to visit Belmont, New York. Or Vermont.

A couple of hours after leaving Belmont, I got lost. Good as my maps were, they did not include every secondary road in upstate New York, let alone the tertiary ones. When I left the Southern Tier Expressway for the last time, it was to drive up the east side of Keuka Lake, which is one of the Finger Lakes, and into a good wine-growing district. I may have missed the Napa Valley; I wasn't going to miss Finger Lakes, too.

At the top of Keuka, there's a town called Penn Yan. From there I meant to drift east to Seneca Lake and up along its shoreline, perhaps tasting the occasional wine as I went. Instead, I got on the wrong road. I drove in a sort of thirty-mile ellipse around Penn Yan, finding whole towns that weren't on my map, such as Dundee, New York, and scaring myself quite a lot. It wasn't the getting lost that scared me; on a sunny afternoon that has a certain interest. It was the behavior of the California truck. Some of the hills on those back roads were very steep indeed, and of course, I was pulling Solo, all 3,300 pounds of him. If I needed to stop at a crossroad, partway down one of those hills; if I even needed to slow down, as twice I did for farm tractors, I was in mortal danger of slewing. I had to play the brakes as carefully as one would a violin.

Going up the hills was even worse. For the first time in the whole trip, Pequop Summit and all, the truck was overheating. By the time I reached the top of each hill, the needle was right on red. I expected the radiator to boil over any minute. By the time I had found where I was, and had started up Seneca Lake toward the pretty town of Geneva on a level road, the needle stayed constantly on red. I was accelerating up to forty-five, cutting the engine, coasting until the speed dropped to thirty, and then turning the engine back on and doing it again. It worked fairly well, though annoying to cars behind me. Fortunately, there weren't many.

Geneva is far bigger than El Paso, Illinois, or Belmont, but still eczema-free. At this moment I wished it weren't. I could have used a motel zone just now. It was getting near dark, and I was tired of waiting for the radiator to erupt. I passed house after beautiful house along the lake, but no motel. I got into the center of Geneva and out the other side. Still no motel. Just the town of Waterloo, New York. By now I was thinking that if I ever got back to open country, I'd park on the edge of a field and sleep on the grass. At that moment I came to the Waterloo Motel. This was no truckers' place with a wide expanse of parking, but a rather small motel. There was no way I could stay here without unhitching. I pulled in anyway.

The tow-bar was still sulky from having been tricked in the morning. It would not release. Only with the help of a man named Chuck Westcott, who checked in just after me, could I get the two vehicles apart. Chuck's young wife clearly thought he might have put in his time better unloading their own car. "Well, look at the Good Samaritan," she said mockingly, as he pried the tow-bar loose.

"You *are* one," I said.

"Glad somebody knows it; *she* don't."

In the morning it took a mechanic from a garage to put the

vehicles back together, and this time I made a serious vow. You two will stay together until we get to Vermont.

By midafternoon, I was in the village of Fonda, New York, headed toward Saratoga Springs. It was fiercely hot. I stopped at a dairy bar for a milk shake lunch. Within minutes a man in an elegant white suit came over to where I was sitting at a wooden picnic table, eating the shake with a plastic spoon. He introduced himself as Levio Lazzari.

"Is that your electric car?"

"Sure is."

"Well, I just wanted to tell you that one of my neighbors has three. He's working to develop an electric car for Ford."

"You mean in Detroit?"

"No, no, right here in Rotterdam, New York. He's doing it *for* Ford, but he works for GE."

At that moment my plans for the day changed. I had been going to Saratoga; now my destination was Rotterdam. Levio Lazzari had given me his neighbor's name; he even knew the phone number. I wished to meet this man.

CHAPTER 16

The Man Who Loved Electric Cars

No pollution, no gas, no oil, no this, no that. I think it's a good idea.
—The owner of Topps Restaurant in Rotterdam, New York, telling his head waitress about the two electric cars he has just been outside to look at.

A BOUT 7:45 on the morning of May 22, 1991, a man in a white electric car drove up to Topps Restaurant in the very center of Rotterdam. His name was Robert D. King. He was an electrical engineer working in the Power Electronics Laboratory of General Electric. He commuted regularly to work in one of the four electric cars he has owned. Three of these cars he built himself. Two of them have been up Mount Washington. One of them has a bumper sticker saying so. All of them avoid pollution.

Bob King built his first EV in 1972, when he was twenty-five. This was a standard heavy car, and no better than Solo at climbing mountain passes. But fine for going to work in.

In 1976, he built another—and this one was designed specifically for going up mountains. It weighed only 1,300 pounds, complete with batteries, and could no more have accommodated passengers or been used for comfortable commuting than the vehicle driven by Jack O'Brien's grandchildren. It couldn't even have passed state inspection as a regular car, since it did not meet safety standards. It could and did glide up the tallest mountain in the East.

His third car, a bright red one, was both heavier and more comfortable. But it was still half a ton lighter than most EVs. It weighed 2,200 pounds, complete with batteries. It met all safety standards. In the summer of 1978, that car, carrying Bob, his wife, Barbara, and their three-month-old son, Stephen, also rolled silently up Mount Washington. Then it rolled down again, making power all the way. This car had regenerative braking. When you stepped on the brake pedal, you didn't just dissipate the car's energy as heat, you converted most of it back into electricity, which got fed back into the batteries. It made enough power coming down to go an extra ten miles after it reached the bottom. In this homemade vehicle Bob commuted to work for nearly ten years, before he bought the white factory-made EV he now uses. Light electric cars are possible, and not just for Chiquita.

Bob drives an EV to work. After he gets there, he is still thinking about EVs. These days his job is to design improved drive trains for them. General Electric is not planning to manufacture an electric car, but Levio Lazzari spoke truly. The Ford Motor Company is. A few years from now, Ford electrics will be—what did that boy in Meadow Vista say?—as common as blackberries. Electric Ford vans went into production in the spring of 1992; electric Ford cars will be along later. Maybe there'll be a famous Model E, standing for electric, environmental, energy-saving, economic, excellent, easy. How involved will General Electric be? "I can't talk about it much," is Bob's answer to all such questions.

But this much is clear. General Electric is going to take a far more vigorous role in the second flowering of EVs than in the first. Back in the first period, many at GE were skeptical about electric buggies and electric surreys, Waverleys and Bakers. In October 1899, for example, Professor Elihu Thomson of GE gave a speech in which he assigned electric vehicles no future at all. The batteries are "an unmitigated nuisance," he said, and what's more, electricity is way too expensive to use driving cars around.

Perhaps it was in 1899—though Professor Thomson's figure of 25 cents a mile for driving an EV baffles me. But electric rates were then dropping rapidly. By 1903, EV owners who had odometers and could therefore keep track of mileage were reporting fuel costs that ranged between 1.5 cents and 4 cents a mile, and those without were reporting monthly electric bills for their cars of $7 and $8. I doubt very much if they were only driving twenty-eight to thirty-two miles.

Actually, Professor Thomson didn't think gasoline cars had much of a future, either. First of all, they were dangerous; gasoline is liable to explode. Here he had a point. Gasoline *is* dangerous, and not just in the way he was talking about. No one was allowed, in those days, to drive a gasoline car either on or off a ferry, for fear it might explode and burn the boat. On many ferries, people had to push the gas cars on and off by hand; the Brooklyn Ferry kept a team of horses at each terminal, to tow them. Electric cars, of course, drove on and off freely.

In 1901, a bill was proposed in New York to forbid the sale of gasoline within the city limits. Everyone knew the bill (which didn't pass) was being pushed by the electric cab companies—but it still reflected a general fear.

Thomson's main point, though, was that gasoline was too scarce to figure as a widespread fuel. Prices had doubled in three years, and if there were a lot of gas cars, would keep on doubling. The future belonged to steam automobiles, said this employee of the largest electrical manufacturing company in the United States. It's the kind of statement that anyone minded to make automotive prophecies does well to keep in mind. Thomson was no fool. He was using the best wisdom of 1899. And he was totally wrong.

Ninety-two years later, in Rotterdam, New York, in 1991, Bob King of GE parked his white electric car next to my red one, and we proceeded to have a look at each other's vehicles, before we went in to get a cup of coffee. I looked first. Like me, he has a twenty-three-horsepower engine, though it's of a different design.

"How fast will yours go?"

"Top speed is sixty-two," he says, "though I once went sixty-five on a slight downhill."

"How many batteries?"

"Eighteen."

How can this be? I wonder. I have looked with real care under his hood, and I haven't seen any batteries at all. Just his motor, his controller, a little tank of something or other, and what looks to be some kind of burner. Solo also has eighteen batteries, and eight of them are right there under the hood. If Bob's car has them all in back, how come the front bumper doesn't stick up in the air like the bow of a canoe when there is a paddler in the stern, and nothing up front?

"Where do you hide them?" I ask.

Bob smiles under his brown mustache. "I'll show you." And only then do I notice that his car has no back seat. It's all batteries where a back seat should be. His are a little smaller than mine. At full charge they're supposed to produce 75 amperes for 106 minutes, while my batteries are supposed to produce the same 75 amperes for 125 minutes.

What do these figures mean? I find it hard to say what *anything* means, electrically speaking. But I'm going to try, all the same.

First I'd better say what an ampere is. Already that's hard. Most of us encounter amperes only as a way of expressing the capacity of an electrical circuit. The typical wiring of an American house has numerous circuits of 15 or 20 amps—and then for the heavy-duty stuff like a clothes dryer, a couple of 30-amp circuits. Try to get a bigger current through, and you blow your fuse or pop your circuit breaker.

Or put it this way. Think of a volt as the driving force of an electric current, and an ampere as the size of the current. A 1-ampere current being driven by 1 volt produces 1 watt. A 10-amp current being driven by 100 volts produces 1 kilowatt. Keep it up for sixty minutes, and you've used a kilowatt-hour.

An electrician would blanch at this description—but consider the alternatives. An ampere can also be defined as one coulomb per second, or as what you get when you send a one-volt current through a resistance of one ohm, or any of several other ways that are perfectly meaningless unless you already understand electricity.

An electric car, of course, needs a much bigger circuit than your beggarly 15 or 30 amps. Try 400. It will need that much only rarely, at maximum acceleration, but even on the sedatest road it will take a lot. And now we get to battery ratings.

Seventy-five amperes is an arbitrary figure picked by battery companies. Well, partly arbitrary. It also reflects actual use by a golf cart, or an EV cautiously driven. If you remember John Fratcher's Jet Electrica, back in Citrus Heights, you'll recall that he had an ammeter—a meter for measuring amperes—on the dash. How I envied him. It could register anywhere from zero (waiting at a red light) to 400 (climbing a steep hill at top speed). But if John were just cruising along at a steady 30 mph, the meter would show around 75 amps.

Turn now to Bob King's car in Rotterdam. That his battery array was rated at 75 amps for 106 minutes meant that he should be able to drive his car at city speeds for about an hour and three-quarters. Provided, of course, he drove up no hills and did no cowboy accelerating. That my array could supply 75 amps for 125 minutes meant that I could drive the same way for just over 2 hours. So now you can calculate our ranges. Not precisely, since you're not taking into account either the voltage or the weight of the vehicles. But roughly. For Bob, multiply 30 mph by 1.75 hours, and you get a city driving range of a little over 50 miles, which is in fact what he has. For me, multiply 30 mph by 2.08 hours. Solo emerges with a city driving range of 62 miles. I've never done any consistent city driving, so can't confirm this from experience, but it sounds about right.

Batteries are tricky things. You might suppose that if my array could supply 75 amps for 125 minutes, it could equally well supply 150 amps for 62 ½ minutes. That is, Solo could go twice as fast for half as long. You'd be wrong. Batteries aren't like that. They have different amounts of power, depending on how fast you draw it out. The more quickly you draw, the less power they will give. An array like Solo's could actually only supply 150 amps for about 52 minutes, and then the juice would be all gone. So if I drive at 60, his range drops to 52 miles. And even that would depend on flat country, no braking, etc.

On the other hand, if you're willing to draw the power really slowly, you get quite a lot extra. Batteries love to dole it out—and when you go slow enough, it's almost like the miracle of the loaves and fishes.

Back in 1902, a British electric car manufacturer sent a car the ninety-seven miles from London to Chippenham on one charge. It was a good car with a good set of batteries. But the main reason for that mighty trip was that the driver went so slowly. He drew an average of only 20 amperes, glided along at ten or fifteen miles an hour, spent all day going the ninety-seven miles. Batteries are like that. It's the other part of the explanation, besides extreme light weight, why Chiquita's and Tracy and Jay's cars could run so long.

But never mind Chippenham. I am still in Rotterdam, New York, outside Topps Restaurant, looking at where Bob King's back seat used to be. Now I wander up and peer under the raised hood again.

"I can identify your motor and your controller," I say, "but what's that?" I point to the little tank.

"Diesel fuel," Bob answers. "I have a diesel heater." He points to the burner thing. "There it is. Keeps me nice and warm. In a whole winter I might burn a gallon or a gallon and a half of diesel oil."

Though this is a sultry May morning, my mind flashes ahead to the cold Vermont winter that's coming. Did I make a mistake, shrugging off so lightly the California doctor's complaint about his inadequate heater?

I know *why* Solo has an electric heater, rather than diesel or propane. Or at least I know the main reason. He was built in California as a zero-emission vehicle. The state regulation that is going to begin requiring such vehicles on California roads by 1998 specifically says that an electric car won't count as zero emission if it has any sort of fossil fuel heater. This has not been a popular requirement with car makers. I've read part of the record of the hearings before the California Air Resources Board, and there were a lot of representatives of the auto industry there, arguing that it wasn't fair to count the little dab of pollution from a diesel or propane heater. This wasn't just Detroit; the Japanese protests were even louder. But the board wouldn't budge.

The auto people then went on to protest, with far greater passion, the similar rule for air conditioning. Their argument was that while a few Californians might buy cars without big comfy heaters, none at all would buy cars without nice cool air conditioning. And if they were to run the cooling systems off the batteries, they'd cut the range by a third. It couldn't work. To which the board answered: Nonsense. Car air conditioners can be made far more efficient than they are now—and cars themselves could be far better insulated. We think you can power the air conditioner of an EV from the batteries without sacrificing more than 10 percent of the range. Zero is going to mean zero.

Well, I feel that way, too. Vermont has no regulations on types of heaters in EVs, and I could install anything the car will accommodate. Maybe the first ten-below day I'll bitterly wish I had. The old Dodge truck was long ago, when I was younger and probably had better circulation. But right now I'm glad I *don't* have a diesel heater. I want to be able to look future Alisons in the eye and not have to confess to any little secrets.

Still talking, Bob and I went on into Topps. There is still much I want to ask him, such as what gears it's best to drive in. The home-made manual that came with Solo said to stay mostly in second and third. You supposedly get better mileage in the lower gears.

"Do *you* always drive in second and third?" I ask.

"Well, first, second, and third. But don't forget, I have a four-speed shift, and your car has five. I think you'll want to use fourth some."

"What about battery life?" I ask. "They told me at Solar Electric that this set would be good for two to three years."

"Three years, if you're at all careful. I have had this car five years, and I'm on my second set. Of course, you don't replace them all at once. This spring I had to replace two. The other sixteen were fine."

"Tell me that thing about regenerative braking again."

"Which thing?"

"About the extra power."

"What I told you is that there's an oddity here. If you put ten percent of the juice back in by regenerative braking, you're probably going to gain twelve or thirteen percent more power. And you get more than the extra mileage. It's good for the batteries—stirs up the electrolyte." (Electrolyte? That's the sulfuric acid in the battery.)

By now it is 8:40, and Bob is looking at his watch. He's already late for work—had meant to leave twenty minutes ago. Whatever he's doing with or for Ford, it's taking a lot of time. Last night he was in his office until midnight, which is why I didn't meet him until this morning. He will be there late again tonight.

Bob gets in the white electric and heads off to Schenectady. I stay a few minutes to chat with the now deeply interested owner of Topps. Then I get in the pickup and resume towing the red electric toward Vermont.

CHAPTER 17

Coming Home

Sit still, and you shall know what driving really is, for
you are in the hands of the famous, the skillful, the
entirely fearless Toad!
—KENNETH GRAHAME, *The Wind in the Willows*

IT IS NOT FAR from Rotterdam to Vermont. Vermont itself is so
small you could stick it in one corner of Nevada, and not even
notice it was there. I'd suggest the west side of Elko County as a
likely spot; then you could tuck Connecticut or Massachusetts in on
the east side of the county. In other words, I could easily have driven
home from Rotterdam in one day.

It was not part of my plan, however, to arrive in Thetford Center,
Vermont, ignominiously towing Solo behind a California truck. My
plan was to arrive driving the electric car at high speed.

I therefore went no more than 150 miles on May 22, and I did
errands as I went. Most notably, I made a long stop in Rutland,
Vermont, at the factory of the G. H. Grimm Company, manufacturers
of maple sugar equipment. I've been wanting a new flue pan for
about five years now, but haven't been willing to pay as much as the
new ones cost. But today, feeling euphoric that Solo was almost
home, I decided to stop and haggle for one. May is the very best
month to haggle for maple sugar equipment—the season is just
over, and no one will be boiling again until next February or March.

The shining stainless steel pans at Grimm's were beautiful, but even a little two-foor by four-foot pan such as I needed cost $868.

"That's kind of steep," I said.

The man at Grimm's led me out back. "Here's one that got a little dent when we had it at the farm show. I'll give you a hundred off. So that's seven hundred sixty-eight."

"Plus tax," I said thoughtfully. Vermont has a 5 percent sales tax.

"I'll cover the tax," he said at once.

The dent was a very small one. I peeled off two of the last three fifty-dollar bills I had taken out to California, and made a deposit on the pan. Then I sauntered off to lunch.

When you leave Rutland, going east, you drive over Mendon Mountain—and for the honor of the East, I have to report that this was the toughest climb of the trip. Up one side and down the other, I drove almost entirely in second gear, and the little truck was straining. It didn't overheat, being freshly supplied with coolant, but it worked its hardest. I was glad enough to stop when I got to White River Junction, twenty miles from home, and spend the night. I got a haircut, had the truck's radio antenna fixed at last, ate dinner at a restaurant I know well. In the late spring evening, at a motel just outside White River Junction, I had the first real talk with a trucker of the whole trip. The drivers were perfectly civil at Burns Brothers and Little America, but they were not inclined to hobnob. If any were interested in Solo, they concealed it beautifully. But now, almost home, I had a long and friendly chat with a driver from Lufkin, Texas, a man who told me with some nostalgia that he spent Christmas Day of 1978 at Little America. He was also openly interested in Solo.

"What'd it cost?" he asked after a while. I told him $17,500.

"And how much e-lectricity does it use in a day?" I told him about $1.50 worth, more if I got a double charge.

"Why, hail, it'll pay for itself in a year." That's rather optimistic, but I liked hearing him say it anyway.

The next morning, May 23, one of our daughters dropped Anne off at the motel. She had come to drive the California pickup one more time, and she emerged from Connie's car holding the largest of our farm pry-bars in her hand. With that, we were easily able to unhitch.

Anne got in the truck, and I got in Solo. In all the long way from Santa Rosa, I had never driven the little car more than about fifty-eight miles an hour. Often there were speed limits, and always I was trying to stretch the range by not going at top speed.

But now I was twenty miles from home, with friends all the way, and my wife right behind in the truck. I didn't think it would be possible to use up the whole charge in twenty miles, except maybe by going continuously up and down Mendon Mountain, or returning to Donner Pass. But if I were wrong, Anne had also brought my big mason's hammer. If necessary, we could even try the O'Brien jump. But it wouldn't be. Solo was going to finish this trip by himself.

Interstate 91 runs from White River Junction to within about three miles of my farm. With a certain wild look in my eye, I drove up the entrance ramp and headed north. A couple of big trucks were coming. I pressed the accelerator pedal to the floor, and shot in ahead of them. Or perhaps I should say I merged smoothly and at high speed into the light morning traffic. Almost at once I was going sixty-five.

This being Vermont, soon there was a hill, and before I reached the top, my speed dropped to fifty-five. Down the other side, however, I picked up to seventy, and that speed I maintained on the level stretch that followed. The California doctor I talked to back in March claimed he'd had his Solar Electric car up to seventy-four, and I see no reason to doubt him. But I have to admit that seventy-one is the fastest I went on my way home. It was enough. Solo shot past a fair number of gasoline cars (most of which shot back past him when we came to the next hill). As for big trucks, I couldn't show them my dust, because there is no dust on I-91. But there were several that I like to think I went by somewhat in the style of a red meteor. And I left not one particle of hydrocarbon in my wake.

Did I use up the whole charge? Certainly not. The gauge was down only three bars when Solo arrived at his new home. Half an hour later I was down in the village, showing him off to people at the general store, collecting my mail, and giving our postmistress a brief ride. She liked the car a lot.

"Well, Ned, when are you going to get your wife one?" she asked.

CHAPTER 18

Solo Becomes a Commuter Car

"It's a toy," said the man with a gasolene machine; "it's a bubble for girls and not a business proposition."
But the little electric took hold of a business proposition such as no gasoline machine in the town had to face, and it took hold with the vim of a polo pony. In fact it was commuting. It went three miles to town every morning, and it came back every night, ending the trip with a climb of a quarter of a mile up a hill.
—FLORA LEWIS MARBLE, "An Electric Automobile in Winter," *Country Life in America,* December 15, 1910.

THE NEXT DAY, May 24, Solo began his career as a commuter car. About 8:00 A.M. I walked out of the house, and over the twenty feet to the barn. The car was sitting out front, soaking up sun with all six solar panels. All night it had been soaking up more from the grid.

I unplugged, got in, and drove to work. Nothing dramatic happened. Plenty could have. There are six different ways I can go to work—and all of them start with a stiff climb. The two ways I most often take both begin by going straight up Thetford Hill, a rise of 420 feet in one mile. Maybe I could have had an ampere problem. But I didn't. I just cruised up the hill, partway down the other side, onto I-91, and headed south to the college. The trip took sixteen minutes. Once there, I parked in a college lot conveniently near my office. If you arrive by 8:20, you can nearly always find a good place. I did not plug in. Couldn't have. There are no outlets in the parking lot.

In midafternoon I drove home again, and pulled up in front of the barn, which faces south. I left the car taking on electricity through its panels, and also through one of the fifty-foot cords. I did not give it another thought until the next day. And that's how it should be with one's transportation. One shouldn't have to worry about it; it should just be there.

Because I wasn't teaching, I didn't go in to the college much that summer. Once, maybe twice a week, I drove in to use the library and to write the reference letters that students and ex-students and middle-aged men and women who were students twenty-five years ago want and need, twelve months a year. In the fall, though I still wasn't teaching (I'm on part-time), I began to go in much more. As I write this chapter, I have taken Solo in to the college just under a hundred times. Nearly all these trips have been boring and uneventful. Well, not boring; the drive is too pretty for that. But without incident.

As for maintenance, there hasn't been much. You are supposed to water the batteries of an electric car once a month, and for the first two months I faithfully did that. They didn't need much. Three quarts each time. Three quarts of distilled water added to eighteen batteries works out to a third of a pint per battery, or a bit under two fluid ounces per cell. Hardly worth taking the caps off. Bob King had told me he watered *his* batteries once every six months—and he's an electrical engineer. I'm not that relaxed yet. But I've slowed my pace to once every couple of months. It takes about twenty minutes.

Twice I've done another bit of maintenance that takes five minutes more. I read in an article about EVs that there is a very slow buildup of sulfuric acid on the tops of the batteries, and that a small leakage of electricity results. I checked with a battery expert, and it's true. To prevent it, you mix a little baking soda with water, and dribble this solution on the tops of the batteries. Twice I've done that. You get a nice fizzy reaction.

I also, remembering John Fratcher's advice, bought a nine-foot cord to use for home charging, and I had a new 20-amp circuit installed at the very front of the barn, so that I could park outside in the sun and still easily plug in. The short cord makes a real difference. With a fifty-footer, charging from that outlet begins at 14 amps. With the nine-footer, it begins at 16.

Have there been repairs? Yes. I had one after just three months. A fuse blew, and I had to replace it. This sounds easier and more casual than the actual event. From my point of view, what happened was that one day in August the car refused to charge. It just wouldn't. I'm no electrical engineer, and I felt the usual helpless anger that nontechnical people experience when some piece of machinery doesn't work. No point in kicking it; I wouldn't even know where *to* kick. What I needed was help.

There are engineering students at the college who know a great deal about electric cars—but they're not around in August. There's a local service station owner named Dave Ring who is in the process of building his own EV—I'd met him in July. But local in this case means fifteen miles away, and besides, he hadn't built it yet. What I thought to do when the car wouldn't charge was to call Solar Electric in California.

"I'm pretty sure it's the fuse in your charging circuit," Neil Sinclair said, and told me how to change it. And then he asked casually, "You haven't been starting your charge on High, have you?" Sometimes I had. I don't any more.

So, for the first six months, the maintenance consisted of watering the batteries four times, and dribbling baking soda on them twice. The repairs consisted of changing the fuse. Did I have no other problems? Yes, I did. I had one concerned with commuting to the college, and one with other use of the car.

The college problem is simply this. Sometimes you don't want to drive in and park, do your work, and then drive home. Sometimes you want to drive in, work, and then use the car for something else before you go home. Maybe run down to Kibby Equipment in White River Junction for a logging chain, or over to a friend's house in Canaan, New Hampshire, for a visit. If it's a very short extra trip, no problem. But if it's more than a few miles, then you start worrying about running out of charge.

The solution, of course, is to plug in while you're at work, so that you leave the college lot with a full charge. This is also better for the batteries. The more you run them off the top half of the charge, the longer they will last. I gather that if you ran them just off the top quarter, they'd be practically immortal.

But in order to plug in, you need an outlet. There are even fewer of these in Dartmouth College's parking lots than there are around Glidden House. Only truck stops are much good for plug-in parking—truck stops and a small but growing number of parking lots in Denmark that are being specially built for electric vehicles. Well, and one other kind of place. I've heard there are some public outlets in very cold cities like Minneapolis and Anchorage, Alaska— not for EVs, but for regular gas cars to plug in and keep their engines warm in winter.

I, of course, needed something in Hanover, New Hampshire. What I did, the first time I had a considerable trip to make, was to park on the street in front of the building where I work, and try to plug in through my office window. No go. I wouldn't have guessed the distance to be more than fifty feet, but it was, and I had only one cord with me.

Occasionally I will do something mildly daring. What I did now was to drive up on the lawn next to my building, and run my cord into the little kitchen on the ground floor. I picked that because the outlet was a three-pronger, and therefore the circuit was almost certainly 20 amps or more.

One of the jobs of Buildings & Grounds people is to protect the lawns. I probably could have been towed, or come out and found a boot on my wheel. Neither of these things happened. The only result of leaving Solo on the lawn that day was that I found a note under the windshield wiper when I came out. "To the owner of this car," it said. "Would you please tell me where and how you got an electric car?" It was from a summer-term student.

The third time I parked on the lawn, however, I provoked a quite different response. It came in an envelope from Buildings & Grounds. A scolding? No, a copy of an anonymous letter they had received. I can't prove it, but I suspect it was sent by one of my four hundred colleagues on the faculty. The style sounds academic. This

is what the anonymous person wrote to Richard Plummer, Director
of Buildings and Grounds:

> Here's a good one for you. Noel Perrin, who now owns an electric
> car and is fond of telling everyone how little it will cost him to drive it,
> just demonstrated what he means by that statement. He pulled his car
> up close to Sanborn (onto the grass, actually) and "plugged it in,"
> using a long extension cord. Well I guess it's going to be inexpensive;
> he's not paying for the electricity to recharge it half the time! The
> College should bill him.

Whoever sent that note did me a favor. I'm not sure he or she
meant to, but that's how it worked out.

Naturally I called Dick Plummer at once, and said yes, it was all
true. I've been on the grass three times, and I took somewhere
around fifty cents' worth of free power each time. I will gladly reform.
If the college would just install an outlet for me in one of the parking
lots, I would never go on the grass again.

"And you'd pay for installing the outlet?" Dick asked.

"Of course."

"Well, I guess we could pay half," he said.

This was wonderful. I had known all along that I'd have to approach the college about a more conventional parking place. Driving up on the lawn next to Sanborn worked just fine in the summer,
but it wouldn't when winter came—too much snow on top of the
grass. And yet winter was when I would most need to plug in. Forget
side trips; I might need a booster charge just to get back to Thetford.
On a zero morning, batteries lose sixty percent of their ability to
hold electricity. On a sub-zero morning, even more.

So why hadn't I forehandedly been making arrangements? Because one big barrier stood between me and a special outlet in a
parking lot, and I hadn't figured out how to get over it. The problem
was this. If the college installed an outlet for Solo, they would also
have to reserve him a parking spot near it. It would do no good at all
if he arrived, and all the parking spaces near the outlet were already
taken.

But the college does not like to provide reserved parking places.

Not counting Handicapped, I doubt there are more than ten on the whole campus. Even the president gave up his a couple of years ago, because parking is so tight. He didn't have to; he's just that kind of man.

What case could I make for getting a privilege that even the president doesn't have? Well, I'd been working on it. My first point was going to be that a precedent existed. Eight or nine of those reserved places are for cars that have to be in and out all day, like the campus police cruisers. But one is for a three-person pool car—and that pool car gets one of the most desirable parking spots at the whole college. Why? Obviously because a three-person pool car saves gas and avoids pollution. So does an EV. One like mine saves more gas and avoids more pollution than a pool car of no matter how many persons. But now comes the weak part of my case. The pool car has another advantage. It frees up two parking places. I couldn't claim that Solo frees up room for so much as a bicycle. If Bill Barr, the head of the parking office, pointed that out, I didn't see how I could answer.

And now I didn't have to. Mr. Plummer had given me a tacit go-ahead, which Mr. Barr promptly confirmed. Within a week I had a reserved place with outlet, and a deal to pay the college $5 a week during terms that I teach, and $2.50 a week during terms that I don't. This winter, the matter of people not getting to use that empty space on days I don't come in will not arise, because my reserved spot is a temporary one, back behind a building, where there's already a three-prong outlet. In the spring the college will install a new one in a regular lot—and I think the deal will be that my place will be reserved only until 10:00 A.M., so that if I don't come in, someone else can have the spot. It'll be the first break late risers have had in years.

All this probably would have happened without the anonymous note. But not so quickly. I am inclined to add the sender of it to my list of providential interveners, like John Fratcher in Auburn and Levio Lazzari in Fonda, New York.

The most cynical of my friends on the faculty, incidentally, predicts that once I get the public reserved place in the regular lot, there will be a sudden rash of EV purchases. People will do anything, she says, for a reserved parking place.

My other problem with the car stems from the kind of marriage I have. Like a good many in the 1990s, it's a commuter marriage. My wife lives in one house, and I live in another. The houses are forty-six miles apart.

At first glance that may seem too small a distance to require a commuter marriage. If a person with a career in Seattle marries a person with a career in Chicago, obviously they either commute or one person subordinates his or her career. But forty-six miles? Anyone can move that far without serious inconvenience. Well, maybe.

Here was Anne's and my problem. When we met, which was only four years ago, we were both deeply settled in: one in Barnet, Vermont, and one in Thetford, Vermont. We each had a house, land, children who liked being where they were. And we had jobs that were farther apart than our houses. Hers took her 15 miles north of her place, to a small school; mine took me 13 miles south of mine, to the college. Had she moved in with me, grumbling kids in tow, her daily round trip to work would have been 122 miles. Had I moved in with her, mine would have been 118. Too far. Someday we'll merge households, but not yet. Meanwhile, we spend time with each other on a schedule that varies every week.

Flash back now to May 1991. The first two nights after I got home with the car, Anne was able to stay in Thetford. The third night I intended to go to Barnet. I had had a blissfully easy commute to the college the day before; now it was time to see what the trip to Anne's would be like. Or, rather, to see if it would even be possible. As I've mentioned, Vermont has a lot of hills.

Just as in going to college, I start out to Anne's by climbing the 420 feet up Thetford Hill. Then I either drop down 520 feet on the other side, and go north on U.S. 5, along the Connecticut River. Or I take I-91. Either way, there are plenty of hills, including a couple of doozies just before I get to Anne's little farm.

I elected to go on the interstate, and I got a good scare right away. Solo charged up Thetford Hill as cheerfully as the day before, but then, only one mile after I got on the interstate, there was a green flash. Great! Forty-two miles to go, and I've already used the best bar. Doesn't look as if I'll make it. I remind myself of the contingency plans.

If things go as badly as they did on Donner Pass, I'll head for the P &
H Truck Stop in Wells River. I can leave Solo plugged in there, and Anne
will come and get me. But that's only thirty miles from home, and it's not
ALL uphill. I still hope to do better than that.

After Wells River comes Barnet village. That's where I get off I-91. If I
have to, I can probably plug in at the Barnet store for an hour, and than
proceed. But the next few miles are fairly level, on up Route 5 to Pass-
umpsic village, just two miles from Anne's. Maybe I can get that far.
There's another general store, and Anne has already arranged with
Lewis, who owns it, for him to leave a heavy-duty electric cord sticking
out under his stockroom door, so that I can get electricity even if the store
is closed. It's settled. I'll park Solo there tonight, and phone Anne for a
ride.

While I'm thinking, I'm also driving. Solo is now doing much
better. He goes eight miles on the second green bar, and I'm safely
past Fairlee. He goes eight more on the third, and I am past Bradford.
But then comes a series of big hills, and the gauge flashes down with
some speed. When I leave the interstate and roll down the one street
of Barnet village, it is just dropping to the last green bar. I glance at
the store, hesitate, and then keep going. That bar's still holding
when I pull up at Lewis's, ten minutes later. Solo has taken me
forty-four up-and-down miles. Good little car. Maybe I'll risk the last
two miles.

I know very well, of course, that the green light is delusive. While
I'm inside calling Anne to tell her my plans, the gauge will drop two,
maybe three bars, and the yellow or red it then shows will be more
accurate than this lovely green. I will not panic, however, the way I
did at Meadow Vista. I also know that if I wait a little, the gauge will
climb back up a bar.

It's 6:55 on a May evening, and still broad daylight. Stranded in
the evening sun? who cares? I go in and call my wife; I tell her I'm
going to try to make it. If I don't show up in half an hour, she's to
come and get me.

While I'm on the phone, the high school boy running the store
strolls out and has a look at Solo. (The store is closing in five minutes, and I'm the only customer.) When I come out, he asks me if I've
seen Hilltopper.

"Seen what?"

"Hilltopper. It's the electric car built last winter by kids at St. Johnsbury Academy. It just won the Tour de Sol."

So there's another EV in Vermont, and I didn't even know it. Well, Anne's place is just four miles from St. Jay; she has a niece in tenth grade at the academy (which is also the town high school). I will make that car's acquaintance.

The gauge is on low yellow when I get back in. But Solo goes easily up the first hill. It turns to red at the foot of the long hill below Anne's house, and that one I go up at about the speed of the man in Rhode Island in 1904. But I do get up it, pick up speed on her driveway, and come gliding up to her barn. I have made the full trip. I made it. If Solo can do this, how easy marital commuting is going to be for EV-owners who live in level places.

That was Saturday. Sunday we took Solo into St. Jay, and he went on back dirt roads with ease. But then came Monday morning, and the return trip to Thetford. My mistake was not to check the voltage before I left. As I now know, it's a slow-charging circuit in Anne's barn.

The trip started out just fine. I zipped down Anne's hill, on through Passumpsic and Barnet villages, onto I-91. I cruised down that at a careful fifty-five, only going up to seventy down hills.

All the same, by the time I neared the rest area above Bradford I was in deep trouble. Last green bar, and eighteen miles to go. In I turned, hoping for a little state electricity. No custodian in sight. An old man drinking a cup of coffee said he was on the other side, mowing grass at the twin rest area over there. I plugged in anyway. Instantly all the lights went out, except a fluorescent one in the ceiling, which must have been on a different circuit. Damn all 10-amp wiring!

"Lucky for you I know where them breakers are," said the old man. I waited, full of apologies, until he had the lights back, then left.

I got as far as Fairlee. There I plugged in for an hour at Newton's Garage, paying a little under one-seventh of what I paid to the Arco station in Fairfield, California. Then I drove comfortably home.

Since then I have taken the car up to Anne's maybe half a dozen times. Sometimes I make it without stopping; sometimes I don't. It depends not only on the state of the charge and the speed I drive at, but also on how warm or cold the weather is, and even a little bit on what everybody from Sacramento on always suspected: whether or not the sun is shining.

If Solo were my only vehicle, this is a style of commuting I could live with. I would just always bring letters to write, or a book to read, in case I had to stop for an hour. Sort of the way I've seen students in a lecture course bring a sketch pad or even the text from another course to class with them, so that if the lecture turns out to be boring, they won't have wasted their time entirely.

But of course I still have the gas-guzzling Toyota truck. Until I sold the California cousin, I in fact had two. It is simpler to take the truck. Solo does what I bought him for, and he does it well and quietly. He is one of the two most innocent cars in Vermont. It would be unreasonable to ask for more.

CHAPTER 19

A Digression on Pollution

Cars are the largest single source of air pollution in the
United States.
—JOHN MOFFET, "The Price of Mobility," 1992

They are responsible for half of all air pollution.
—WOLFGANG ZUCKERMANN, *End of the Road,* 1991

I CALL SOLO INNOCENT. Obviously I mean in terms of pollution.
All through this book I have taken it for granted that electric cars
run more cleanly than gasoline or diesel vehicles, even when the
electrics get all their power from the grid. But how much more?

Some people think a lot. The California Air Resources Board, for
example, has said in a somewhat roundabout way that, mile for mile,
EVs that charge from power plants cause less than one-eighth the
damage that gasoline cars do.* The giant California utility, Pacific

*The claim goes like this. The board has set out a sort of base pollution rate—
namely, what will be allowable in a standard 1993 gasoline car sold in California.
Starting in 1994, the board is going to require that at least 10 percent of new
cars each year be what it calls Transition Vehicles. They will be allowed to produce
only half the hydrocarbon pollution of the standard 1993 models. Then in 1997 the
board will get much tougher. At least 25 percent of new cars sold that year must be
Low Emission Vehicles. These will be allowed to pollute only half as much as the
Transition Vehicles. And 2 percent of the 1997 cars must be Ultra Low Emission
Vehicles: "half the levels from the group above."
A half of a half of a half is one-eighth. So with complicated exceptions for certain
emissions, the Ultra Low Emission Vehicles or ULEVs will pollute only one-eighth as

Gas & Electric, goes further still. They have published figures assert-
ing that an electric van "reduces emissions of hydrocarbons by 99
percent, nitrogen oxide by almost 80 percent, and carbon monoxide
by 97 percent." They are counting in emissions from the power
plant.

Not everyone agrees with these cheerful assessments. The EPA,
for example, has big doubts about how much gain there is in shifting to electric cars. Yes, there'll be a lot less hydrocarbons. But there
will also be "a rather dramatic increase in pollutants not normally
associated with the automobile, mainly sulfur dioxide coming from
coal-fired power plants."

When you look at what even quite careful journalists have to say,
you find them divided in the same way. For example, in February
1991 *U.S. News & World Report* published an article on electric cars.
It called them even more innocent than the California Air Resources
Board had dared to. "The vehicles themselves don't pollute at all and,
even when the emissions from power plants used to charge the
batteries are considered, an electric car adds less than 5 percent of
the pollution of a typical gasoline-powered car."

About two months later, on April 1, *Newsweek* offered a radically
different view of electric cars. *Newsweek* felt they were even guiltier
than the EPA had suggested. "How electric cars will affect air pollution depends on where their electricity comes from. If they're
plugged into an outlet where the electrons come from burning coal,
the effects on smog, ozone and the greenhouse will be worse than
from gasoline cars. If the power derives from natural gas, solar, or

---

much as standard 1993 gas cars sold in California.

Now turn to the public hearings that the board held. These are the same hearings at which many automobile companies protested the banning of diesel heaters in
zero-emission vehicles.

Volkswagen (seconded by the Environmental Defense Fund) then pointed out
that zero-emission cars aren't really so zero, anyway. "We cannot ignore the emissions from power plants," they said.

To this the board answered two things. First, that there are also emissions from
gasoline refineries. Second, even when you do factor in power plants, "emissions per
electric vehicle are still substantially lower than the ULEV standards."

So, less than an eighth.

hydro, the car will become less of an environmental villain." But still a villain.

One month after that, in May, *Popular Science* published an article on electric cars which took still a third view. Here the EV emerges neither as hero nor as sinner, but as neutral. "Although an electric car by itself does not pollute, in reality it displaces, rather than eliminates, air pollution to the location where the electric power is generated, particularly when the primary source of electricity is a coal-fired generating plant."

Just what Rod said, back in Laramie. If I believed it, I would junk Solo tomorrow. Reduce my driving range to fifty miles, just to shift a little pollution from Thetford to Rutland, or maybe to the Grand Canyon? No thanks.

How can three responsible magazines come up with three such different conclusions? How can the Air Resources Board see one picture, and the EPA another? It's easier than you might think. One side is concentrating on hydrocarbons, and the other side on sulfur dioxide and particulates. But even beyond that, there's the very nature of environmental studies. Any careful assessment is fantastically complicated—and is apt to depend in part on assumptions, projections, extrapolations, attempts to quantify the almost unquantifiable. Hence the unresolved arguments about cloth vs. disposable diapers, plastic grocery bags vs. paper ones, landfills vs. incinerators. Of course, there are clear-cut cases, too. There is no doubt whatsoever that chlorofluorocarbons are terrible for the atmosphere, and the faster they stop being released from old refrigerator coils, the better it will be for life on this planet. There is no doubt that eating fish that have been contaminated with mercury makes people both sick and crazy. No doubt that asbestos fibers are bad for human lungs.

But these are simple matters compared to an assessment of cars. Suppose you were making a study of car pollution. For the moment you ignore diesels, cars powered on methanol, a.k.a. wood alcohol (of which a few already exist), cars powered on natural gas (many more of these), and hybrids. You just take an electric car and a gasoline car, and set them side by side. Then you start figuring out how much each one pollutes.

For the electric, you might start with the factory where it was built. You wouldn't find much there, since nearly all present EVs are converted gas cars, and the conversion is a fairly clean process. So, go on back to when the gas car was built, and to the steel mills, paint factories, etc., behind that. Now you've got a good bit, though it's only a one-time charge.

Okay, next to the batteries. They will be lead-acid for 95 percent of current EVs. Figure how much of the lead had to be mined, and how much comes from recycling. Take a look at how sulfuric acid is manufactured, and also at what those battery cases are made of.

Batteries are not a one-time thing. As Bob King said, their life expectancy in an EV is two to three years. I'm hoping for a full three years with Solo's, because of his solar panels, but I won't *know* until 1994.

What happens then? Then those sixteen or eighteen batteries are scrapped. Half a ton of scrap. In some cases the used batteries will find their way to a lead-recycling plant in this country, and they will be processed with the merest trace of pollution. In others they will get shipped to third-world processing plants (not necessarily owned by third-world people), and there cause quite a lot.

You still have the tires to think about. They will also need to be replaced, and the old ones will almost certainly not be recycled, even though each one contains a gallon and more of reclaimable petroleum.

All of that is just warm-up. You're finally ready to think about the serious matter, which is fuel. If the electric car you've got up on the stage is going to run on absolutely typical American electricity, you're going to figure that 57 percent of its charge will come from coal-fired generating plants, some low sulfur, some high. Then 20 percent from nuclear plants, 9 percent from natural gas, 8 percent from dear clean hydro, 5 percent from oil, and 1 percent from a combination of wood-burning plants, solar thermal, wind, and panels like the ones on my barn.

Only that's not a sufficiently complicated way to figure. Most EVs are commuter cars, and most of them do their recharging at night. Even Solo, with his plug-in spot behind the Murdough Center at

Dartmouth College, still gets more than half his power at home at night.

Nighttime is when most utilities have surplus generating capacity, and they are free to use their least-polluting plants. Free to, and some actually do. You'll remember that that was part of my answer to Rod—that California could charge up a million or so EVs at night, using local power plants that burn relatively clean natural gas.

So for special EV electricity, you need to cut the coal-fired share down a little from 57 percent, and raise the natural gas share up a little from 9. And that helps, though not enough. You still wind up with a massive quantity of pollution caused by the production of electricity for EVs, even though they're zero emission when you drive them. I can be more precise—and will be in a minute.

Meanwhile, look at the gasoline car. There it stands, guilty and trembling. It is powerful, it is often beautiful, and unless you're incredibly careless, it never runs out of gas during a forty-six-mile drive to your spouse's house. But what a polluter!

Never mind for the moment all that stuff spewing out its tailpipe. Before you even get to that, you've got to consider pollution in oil refineries, as the California Air Resources Board said. Yes, and also tanker spills, and what that redheaded kid spilled on the ground in the filling station in Wyoming, not to mention what car owners themselves spill at the self-serve island. Possibly you should even count last year's fires in Kuwait. No, you definitely should. If all American cars were electric, we wouldn't need one drop of Kuwaiti oil. Nor would we be buying from Saudi Arabia, Iraq, or Libya. And, incidentally, Israel would have no rich enemies.

Shall we glance at the car itself? First, let's consider the catalytic converter. What does it take to manufacture eight or ten million of them a year, so there can be one on every tailpipe? Can *they* be recycled? Are they? Oh, and what about used motor oil? Nobody knows how many millions of gallons of it get dumped annually in the United States, nor what share of this soaks into the ground, and what share dribbles into streams and rivers. There are some good guesses, though, and they all run high.

Don't stop yet. There's still antifreeze to consider (do you have any idea what's *in* that stuff?), and the chlorofluorocarbons in the car air conditioners, and the same questions of steel and paint and plastic that there are with EVs. Only then is it time to talk about the actual emissions from the tailpipe: the carbon monoxide, the hydrocarbons, the particulates, and so forth.

What does it all add up to? For gasoline cars I have a fairly authoritative figure. It comes from John Moffet's groundbreaking study called "The Price of Mobility," published by the Natural Resources Defense Council in 1992. That study is subtitled "The Full Costs of Transportation in the U.S.A." It is the first attempt I have ever seen to put accurate dollar amounts on what it costs to run a train, a bus, a car, a subway. Not just the obvious costs, like buying diesel fuel for the locomotive, or excavating for the subway, but *everything*. That includes the costs of dealing with whatever pollution that form of transportation creates. Gasoline cars, as you may suppose, create the most. Moffet concludes that a gasoline car is responsible for between 4 and 8 cents' worth of pollution for every mile it is driven. Buses pollute 2 to 4 cents' worth per passenger mile, and trains 1.5 to 2 cents' worth.

What about electric cars? Moffet does not consider them separately. But it is possible to do some extrapolating from his Table 17, "Transportation Emissions by Mode." When you do, electric cars charging from the grid turn out to be stunningly better in some ways (they create less than half a percent as much carbon monoxide, for example), moderately better in others, and much worse about sulfur dioxide. Add it all up, and it looks as if an electric car pollutes at most half as much as a gasoline car, probably more like a third or a quarter. That is a huge and wonderful gain. And yet—such a car is still harming the environment at a rate of more than a cent a mile. That's not good enough for us eager purists. Something better is needed.

Okay, stagehands. Push a third car onto the stage. Why, it's Solo! And the stagehands aren't pushing. They don't need to. They can just lounge around and watch, as British stagehands must have in 1895, when Cinderella drove her EV onto a London stage. I'll bring Solo on myself.

Solo does not get any of his power from coal-fired generating plants; there is no sulfur dioxide associated with *him*. Neither does he get any from oil-fired plants, natural gas-fired, or nuclear. He gets every watt from his own six panels, and from the twenty-eight on my barn. This has been true since the moment he and I left Santa Rosa.

You perhaps doubt that? You recall that I plugged in at a pergola in Cleveland, at my own office at Dartmouth, at numerous motels? True. But think of that as like using a credit card. I borrowed power in Cleveland, and it very likely was power made with coal. But I have repaid the grid watt for watt with pollution-free power made by photovoltaic cells. I have usually paid back on the same day I borrowed. Solo is a clean car. His pollution costs might be a tenth of a cent a mile. Before I draw up the balance sheet, though, you need to meet the panel array he relies on. Turn the page.

CHAPTER 20

Entering the Electricity Business

The United States and Switzerland have laws which
require the central utility to provide power to a customer with a PV generator when the sun does not
shine, and to purchase power from the customer's PV
generator when there is excess solar-generated electricity.

—PAUL MAYCOCK, *Proceedings,* Solar and Electric
Vehicle Symposium, 1991

Thetford Center, Vermont, February 15, 1991. It's snowing lightly this
morning, from a pale gray sky. Hardly the day for making solar electricity—and some think Vermont is hardly the place. A long sunny day in
New Mexico would be more like it. Sure enough, at 11:00 A.M. the solar
panels on my barn are producing only 70 watts.

February 16, 1991. The sky is blue this morning, and the recently
risen sun is bright. It's still winter, though. At 8:30 A.M., the thermometer on the front porch reads five above zero. Hardly suntan weather.
And sure enough, the solar panels on my barn are producing only 320
watts.

February 18, 1991. Another sunny day. The panels may not do much
at 8:30, so early in the year, but they gain fast. At 9:00 A.M. I am making
600 watts. At 10:00 A.M. the little display screen in the kitchen reads
820. It flicks down to 810 as a thin wisp of cloud passes near the sun,
flicks back to 820, jumps to 830. For a few minutes around noon,
production reaches 1,000—that is, the panels are making a full kilowatt.

March 5, 1991. The sun has climbed slightly higher and gotten slightly stronger as we near the equinox, but that doesn't explain today's readings. The air must also be exceptionally clear. For a brief period at noon today the panels were making 1,480 watts. That's only 20 watts less than their rated capacity. Today I will supply my own house for a full seven hours. I will also sell 4, maybe 5 kilowatt-hours of electricity to Vermont's largest utility.

THE STORY of how I come to be selling power to the power company begins in the spring of 1990. I had made the decision to look for an electric car, and I was thinking about power sources for it. I considered putting up a windmill and making electricity that way. Problem: There's just not enough wind in our valley. I toyed with a little hydroelectric project. But there's really not much you can do with a brook so small it dries up in June. I thought about just using off-peak power from the local utility, which is called Central Vermont Public Service. It would certainly be cheaper and probably be cleaner than their on-peak power. But not clean enough, I feared, to impress the stern judges in Environmental Studies 1.

Finally I thought about solar panels. Yes! Anyone who has access to the sun can use *them.* At that moment my project was born.

A few days later I went to see a friend who already had solar panels. Such people are fairly common now. I know of eight in this one small section of Vermont with maybe 5,000 inhabitants. You just don't see them often, because they live off the main roads—so far off that there aren't even any power lines. That's why they got solar panels in the first place.

My friend liked her system. A lot. She and her husband and their three-year-old son live in a newly built house which happens to be four-tenths of a mile away from the nearest electric line. They originally planned to bring in power from that line—and were stunned to find that this would cost them $9,500. Around here the cost of bringing in power averages $24,000 a mile if it's a joint operation with the phone company and if the poles are reasonably easy to set. If it's not a joint operation and if the poles are hard to set, the cost will be $36,000 a mile or possibly even more.

So what Sue and Dean did instead was to order an $8,800 solar panel system. For that they got twelve 53-watt panels to go on the roof, twelve deep-cycle batteries to go in a closet, and an inverter to turn the direct current the panels make into alternating current. Plus a control panel, lots of hardware, and an eighty-page assembly manual. All this came from a company called Solar Works, in Montpelier, Vermont.

Sue is about as mechanical as I am, and Dean is an actual klutz. (Good wood-splitter, though.) They didn't even consider putting the system together themselves. They paid Solar Works $1,200 to install it for them, which brought the cost up to $10,000.

A twelve-panel system doesn't produce anywhere near as much electricity as the average American family uses. But then, it doesn't need to. One of the big current-eaters in an American house is the refrigerator. Sue and Dean have a special kind called Sun Frost, which merely by being extraordinarily well made uses one-sixth the power of a standard model. (Typical sixteen-cubic-foot frost-free refrigerator: 120 kilowatt-hours a month. Sun Frost refrigerator, sixteen-cubic-foot model: 20 kilowatt-hours a month.)

Another big user is the hot-water tank. Sue and Dean have a solar hot-water heating system. They got that from Solar Works, too. And that's only a start. They have also installed compact fluorescent lights, which use 18 watts of power but give as much light as an old-fashioned 75-watt bulb. It's not ugly light, either, but pleasing to the eye. This is true. I know. I use those bulbs myself. They have even bought a little backup generator, so that when there's a week of cloudy weather in the winter, they'll still have electricity. And so that Sue can occasionally run a clothes dryer, that most prodigal of American appliances. (How prodigal? Try this for size. A dryer takes 5,000 watts to run—one hour with it on and you've used 5 kilowatt-hours of electricity.) Last winter Sue averaged three gallons of gas a week, running the generator. That's part of her contribution to pollution.

Sue encouraged me to go ahead and get solar panels. "But it's going to cost you money," she immediately added. "You're already hooked up to Central Vermont. They can sell you power a lot cheaper than you can make it with panels."

This is true. Just how true you'll find out shortly. But remember, my goal was to get rid of guilt feelings when I went in to teach Environmental Studies 1. I know people who fork over $100 to a therapist three times a week, hoping to get rid of guilt feelings. If they go for a year, they spend $15,000. And *worth* it, if they eradicate the guilt. I hoped to eradicate mine—and also accomplish something I'd be unlikely to in a therapist's office—namely, to produce a real and measurable reduction in pollution.

Sue had been happy with Solar Works. So the next day I called Montpelier. Leigh Seddon, who runs the company, drove down to look my place over. At first he thought I wanted to quit the power company, even though Central Vermont's lines go right down the paved road in front of my house. He took a look at the mass of electric appliances in the house, and began rapidly figuring how many panels and how many batteries I'd need to run all that.

"Hold on," I said. "I don't want to leave CV, and I don't want to buy batteries. I want to hook up.".

"You mean an interconnect?"

"Yes. I have this vision. Nights I'll buy power from them, same as I do now, and the meter will spin forward. But days—sunny ones, anyway—they'll buy power from me, and the meter will get driven backward. I like that idea."

Leigh frowned a little. He said that as far as he knew, no solar producer had a hookup with CV, and the company might or might not be willing. It's a little tricky, he said, taking the direct current produced by photovoltaic panels and not only turning it into AC, but giving it just the right wave characteristics and just the right voltage so that it can hop into the wires and be compatible with the rest of the company's power. "But no harm asking," he concluded.

So we asked. And CV turned out to be very receptive. Inverters exist, their engineers said, that can turn your kind of power into our kind. Design a good system, and we can probably hook you right on.

Leigh started designing. He quickly discovered one constraint. The sophisticated kind of inverter we'd need doesn't come in tiny sizes. The smallest one requires 1.5 kilowatts of peak power. To produce that, I would need twenty-eight solar panels on the roof, not the puny twelve that Sue and Dean have. Each 53-watt panel would set me back $331—over $9,000 for the whole array. The high-tech inverter would cost another $3,500. I wouldn't have any batteries to buy (until I got my car), but I would need a new breaker panel, etc. etc. And unless I wanted to spend a lot of time teetering on the barn roof, having first become an expert wirer, there would be a several-thousand-dollar installation charge.

Two days later he gave me an estimate: $18,000 for the whole project. I accepted.

The next step was to drive to Rutland and have a formal meeting with Central Vermont. Five utility officials sat around a big table with Leigh and me, and we discussed every aspect of an interconnect. There were no serious problems, just one minor disappointment. I learned from Rick Hackett, a young meter engineer, that my fantasy of driving the meter backward on sunny days wasn't going to work. Because of the complicated rate structure, CV wanted two meters: an incoming meter for power I bought and an outgoing meter for power I sold. That one I would personally own. I'd read it once a month, as meter readers do, and send CV a bill.

Peter Lind, the man in charge of the meeting, then produced a copy of the contract the company uses when buying power from small hydro producers. And now a problem did appear. Article 16 of that contract requires the small producer to carry five million dollars' worth of liability insurance. High-voltage electricity is dangerous stuff. But considering that half an hour earlier Peter had guessed that my monthly income from CV would be in the three- to six-dollar range, the extra premium began to look steep.

Blessings on the high-tech inverter. The one we planned to use is so smart it instantly shuts itself off if it detects a problem. The danger is minimal. In the end Peter managed to get Article 16 modified so that it reads "adequate insurance coverage." My $300,000 homeowners policy counts as adequate.

That meeting took place in September 1990. By mid-October a crew from Solar Works was up on the barn roof mounting panels. When the people who built that barn around 1840 faced it due south, they can't have known how convenient they would be making things for a small energy producer 150 years later. That's the ideal way for any photovoltaic system in the United States to face. It would be better still, of course, if the panels could pivot, following the sun across the sky like a huge sunflower—but that's asking a lot of a barn roof.

Because of the Gulf War, I didn't start making electricity until February 1991. Some of the circuitry used in a smart inverter also gets used in smart weapons, and the delivery date got pushed back three times. At least that gave me plenty of time to think of a name for my little generating station. Not that I named it in the same spirit that an Englishman names his country place. I had to. CV requires a business name for every station it buys power from, even us midgets. Mine is called Thetford Sun Power.

Start-up day did finally arrive—and with it one more problem. It was wonderful to see the inverter come to life. It was wonderful to see the little display screen instantly report that the panels were making power, and to know that for the first time in the house's history it was self-sufficient in electricity, even if only until midafternoon.

But I had not anticipated the noise. Maybe you've walked by an electric substation and noticed the assortment of little squeals and crackles that come from the transformers. My inverter wasn't squealing or crackling, but it definitely chirped. Quite loudly, too. The very next day I had its closet lined with acoustical wallboard, and that has cut the loudness by about two-thirds. You now hear it only in the kitchen. And this faint chirping I have gotten fond of. If I happen to be in the kitchen when the first rays of the sun strike the panels in the morning, I rush over to see how many watts I'm making. Makes mornings twice as interesting as when I just looked at the thermometer on the front porch to see how cold it got.

A month went by, and I received my first check as a producer of electricity. It was for $4.67. I also got my first bill from CV since I joined them in the utility business. That was for $57. Down from $70 the month before. No big deal, but worth having.

In my first year as a producer, I sold CV a little over 1,400 kilowatt-hours, and supplied my own house with around 500. I have, of course, bought a great deal more than that from CV. I don't have a Sun Frost refrigerator (yet), nor a solar hot-water heater. I do have a dryer.

On May 2, when I bought Solo, all that became irrelevant. From that moment to this, the full production of Thetford Sun Power—what I use and what I sell—has been dedicated to keeping Solo on the road. It has been enough, though none too much.

How far will 1,900 kilowatt-hours take Solo? Well, I recently met a North Carolina scientist who drives a Solar Electric car very similar to Solo. He tells me that at highway speeds I should figure 3 miles to the kilowatt-hour. I have a friend in New Hampshire, a solar engineer. He has actually tested Solo going at town speeds—that is, 30 mph. Rob says at that speed figure him at 5 miles to the kilowatt-hour.

About 90 percent of Solo's driving is making commuter trips at high speeds. The other 10 percent is bopping around town at low speeds. For that mix of driving, 1,900 kilowatt-hours gives Solo a yearly allowance of 6,080 pollution-free miles. Plus what his own six panels make. The people at Solar Electric told me to figure one kilowatt-hour on a sunny day, but I think they may have been a little optimistic. Anyway, there are lots of cloudy days in Vermont. So I am going to figure a modest 150 kilowatt-hours for the year, which is an additional 480 miles. Total pollution-free driving allowance: 6,560 miles. That is enough for his commuting and bopping.

If Solo's range were greater, and I could take him regularly up to Anne's, it would not be enough, and I'd have to agonize over whether to enlarge the solar array. As for people with long commutes and cross-country vacation habits who put on 20,000 or 30,000 miles a year, they may smile at the thought of a car whose yearly total is so small. I have a reflection to offer them. It is precisely in the kind of short-range driving I do with Solo that gas cars commit their worst sins. If you take a gasoline car on a long trip, it does not pollute nearly as much per mile as when it is being used for errands. The worst pollution occurs at two points: during the first 5 miles of a trip, and after you stop, while the engine is cooling.

But don't take my word for it. The California Air Resources Board has a whole booklet—I'll be glad to lend it to you—documenting this sort of thing. For example, here's a comparison they make between a gasoline car going fast on a clear road and one going stop-and-start during rush hour. "A car that takes 30 minutes to drive 10 miles will produce two and a half times more pollution than a car making the same trip in only 11 minutes." (Why 11? They mean, at 55 mph.)

Solo, of course, is responsible for the same minuscule amount of pollution either way. If *he* gets caught in traffic, he simply shuts down. The motor, that is. He'll keep the radio playing or the heater heating, and if I had air conditioning, he'd run that. He does the dirty work, and he does it cleanly.*

If Solo were just the expensive toy of a mildly eccentric college professor, that wouldn't prove much. However concerned about the environment they were, no car owner could power an EV from a home solar array unless that person had (a) a sunny roof to mount the array on, and (b) a spare eighteen thousand dollars to pay for it. Only a minority have both those things. I didn't, either, while my daughters were in college.

There's an answer here. Solar panels are not limited to home systems. In a few years it will be possible to get the first small supplies of pollution-free solar electricity right from a power company. At this very minute, an organization called PV-USA is conducting some rather large-scale tests. That name stands for Photo-Voltaics: Utility Scale Application, and it's a joint venture of several utilities

*As he is driven, zero emission. As his electricity is made, zero emission.

Suppose you go back another step. What about when the panels that make his electricity are made? Yes, here there is pollution. My panels come from a company called Solarex, in Maryland. Each one takes several hundred kilowatt-hours of electricity to produce. Solarex makes a few of those hours from a thousand-foot wall at the factory that is completely covered with solar panels. But well over 90 percent comes straight from the grid. I'm afraid coal-fired generators can be seen lurking in the background.

They won't lurk forever. A solar panel has an extremely long life. Somewhere between thirty and fifty years, I've been told. It will take my panels about five years to pay the world back for the energy needed to create them. Then, far into the twenty-first century, they will be making power that owes no debts to anyone.

What that will leave for Solo's daily pollution will be a small pro rata amount for his own manufacture, and a somewhat larger amount for the making and periodic replacing of his tires and batteries. And the battery share may one day dwindle, as you'll hear in the next chapter.

Meanwhile, speaking for the non-existent Vermont Air Resources Board, I'm going to say that Solo's current total pollution is not more than 2 or 3 percent that of a standard gas car. It might even be less.

and several government agencies. In the present first stage, they are testing many different kinds of solar panels—and making considerable power in the process. Thetford Sun Power has a rated output of 1.5 kilowatts. PV-USA has ten arrays of 20 kilowatts each, two of 200 kilowatts, and one biggie of 400 kilowatts. Altogether, that's a megawatt.

These are real-world tests, too. For example, a couple of the twenty-kilowatt systems are being built by Pacific Gas & Electric in the little town of Kerman, California. The Kerman substation is no longer adequate, and the company hopes it might actually save money by making the extra power right on the spot rather than building a new substation. Next year Kerman will be a good place to have an electric car.

This cheery news is an exception, I admit. Solar panels remain very expensive. There seems little prospect that they are suddenly going to get much cheaper—and perhaps none at all that in a few years they'll be able to undersell electricity made from coal. But even here there's hope. All over the world people are working on new kinds of solar technology. One place I've heard a good deal about is Dallas, Texas. There Texas Instruments is busy working on what they hope will be a kind of roll roofing that makes electricity from the sun. If they succeed, their product will operate at a far lower efficiency than the hard silicon panels on my barn. But if the rolls are cheap enough, who cares? Roofs are big places.

Quite apart from photovoltaics, there's another way of getting clean power from the sun. It's called solar thermal. I don't pretend to understand much about it. I understand this much, though. Southern California Edison is currently getting 2 percent of its power from a very large solar thermal installation in the Mojave Desert. Take heart, prospective EV owners. Clean power is on the way.

CHAPTER 21

The Boxborough Exposition

But when it came to getting a modern electric vehicle out of the laboratory and on the road, as a practical, convenient, comfortable, mass-produced car or truck that people would want to drive day in and day out ... well, we just hadn't figured out how to do that.
—ROBERT STEMPEL, chairman of the board, General Motors, 1991

IN LATE OCTOBER 1991 I hitched Solo up for the first time since our arrival home in May. The actual hitching was no problem. John Poor at Thetford Auto had long since hammered out the tow-bar so that it fitted perfectly.

The problem was that I didn't want to tow. I was taking Solo to a combined electric car and solar energy symposium in Boxborough, Massachusetts, near Boston. Among other things, I would be Solar Electric's representative. Not for pay; for the good of electric cars. It would be far more dignified, I thought, for Solo to arrive under his own power, rather than trailing behind a pickup.

But Boxborough is 130 miles from my farm, and there are numerous hills en route. If I just hopped in Solo and left, it would be a two-day trip. The symposium was on Saturday and Sunday. I'd need to leave Friday noon. First drive 50 miles, then hang out somewhere in central New Hampshire until evening, while Solo recharged. Then another 50 miles to a motel. On Saturday morning do the last bit to

Boxborough. No. I wasn't willing to spend that much time.

What about towing Solo just the first 100 miles, and then leaving the pickup in one of those ride-share parking lots? That would ensure a dignified arrival—and it would save about three gallons of gas. It would also, however, be quite misleading. I sighed, and decided to tow all the way.

When I pulled into the parking lot of the Boxborough Host Hotel at 10:00 o'clock on Saturday morning, there were already hundreds of gasoline cars parked in it—and down near the exhibition hall, a knot of four or five electric cars. When I hurried into the hall, there were eight more in there, plus an electric pickup and an electric van. Hundreds of people were looking at them.

"You're late," said Nancy Hazard, the intrepid young woman running all this. She showed me where my car was supposed to go. I went back out, unhitched Solo, and drove him quietly into the hall, nosing past a clump of round tables where people were drinking coffee. I pulled up by a box of brochures Solar Electric had sent from California. Even before I got out, a middle-aged couple came over to ask questions. Between answers I looked around. This was a big hall. Besides the cars, there were thirty or forty booths, practically all belonging to virtuous organizations. The Sierra Club had one. So did the Union of Concerned Scientists, the New England Electric Auto Association, the Northeast Sustainable Energy Association, and so on.

And the hall was just a beginning. The hotel proper was full of EV people attending meetings. At any given moment there were apt to be three symposia going on: one for beginners, one for advanced EV builders, and one on theory. You could get basic instruction on how to convert your old guzzler for a few thousand dollars, or you could get recondite information about secondary lithium batteries.

There were also several plenary sessions that everybody went to. The speaker at the first of these was a man more usually associated with gasoline cars: Robert Stempel, chairman of the board of General Motors. (He wasn't the only head of a car company there, either. James Worden, founder and president of Solectria was also there. So was Douglas Cobb, founder and president of the Solar Car Corporation. These two EV companies are, to be sure, a bit smaller than GM.

They're more the size of Oldsmobile in 1900, which was the year that Ransom Olds built a few electric Oldsmobiles.)

Mr. Stempel gave a good talk. He did not mention the thing I most hoped he would—namely, the date on which GM would begin to sell electric cars. But he brought up lots of interesting things. For example, he said firmly that GM wasn't going into the electric car business to cash in on the California zero-emissions rule. It was the other way round. The Air Resources Board dared to make the rule partly because it knew of GM's plans. "We've heard that the GM announcement [of its commitment to build EVs] encouraged California to mandate the sale of zero-emission vehicles." And he said GM now *had* figured out how to make a practical, convenient, comfortable electric car—though not, of course, one with the range of its gas cars. Go on, I thought. Do it. Later I heard a rumor that they might get into production in the fall of 1993.

I didn't get to many of the symposia, because I was so busy showing Solo off. After lunch, I even backed out past the tables and let three sets of possible EV-buyers take test drives. Then I nosed back inside, put a stack of brochures on his hood, and went off to explore. I was dying to see the other EVs. Doug Cobb had brought two Solar Cars up from Florida. Jim Worden, close by in Arlington, Massachusetts, had come with six Solectrias. They would be the first rival makes that I had a chance to examine.

I liked both. In one respect, I liked them better than my own vehicle. Solar Car and Solectria both make cars with a space-age touch that Solo lacks. Their solar panels are of the new flexible type that can be molded to a curved surface. They thus fit on the roofs and hoods of cars with real elegance. Solo's hard crystal panels are mounted sort of the way a luggage rack is. They sit an inch or two above the roof on little aluminum legs. This not only has an old-fashioned look, it creates a shallow wind tunnel between the panels and the roof of the car, and cuts Solo's range. Not by much. One of the student engineers at Dartmouth guessed it might be 2 percent. I still begrudge it.

The other thing I envied was the instrumentation. All these cars had running ammeters, like John Fratcher's. Some of the Solectrias also had a fuel gauge that was said to be accurate—miles better than my green-yellow-and-red-bar device. I was all set to buy one until I learned the price: $449. That news convinced me to wait a little, in case Solectria should have a sale one day.

The ammeter was another matter. I bought one from Doug Cobb that afternoon for $55. He obviously couldn't install it then and there—you have to put a shunt into the wiring, and do various other time-consuming things. I tossed it on Solo's back seat, planning to have it installed when I got home. It's a measure of something that I never considered locking Solo thereafter, any more than he considered locking up his display of instruments that night. The exhibition hall was dark and empty when I took a look in at 11:00 P.M. And as far as I could tell, everything in every booth was still laid out where it had been. (What was *I* doing in there? Making sure no one had unplugged Solo. I might be giving more rides tomorrow.)

You may wonder why I waited until now to look at the rival makes, rather than back when I was car hunting. There's an excellent reason. I couldn't find either one back then.

The Solar Car Corporation existed, all right. It went into production in January 1991, just about the time I began negotiations with Dick Frost. But I didn't know that. I had never heard of the company. By the time I did hear, I had already sent Solar Electric half the money for Solo, and was beginning to plan my cross-country drive.

I did know about Solectria, and I knew long before Dick Frost made his first phone call. Early in the car search, in April, 1990, I heard a vague rumor that some young MIT graduate was going to start making electric cars down in Massachusetts. No one could tell me his name, or the name of the company, or anything like that. But in early May I got hold of a one-page brochure for the electric car race called the American Tour de Sol. The race would be May 23–27. On May 25 the cars would be passing within ten miles of my house—and not only passing, but stopping at the Lake Morey Inn.

The brochure included brief descriptions of four of the entries. One car was called the Sunrise. The brochure said it was a "2-seater prototype commuter car," made by Solectria Solar Racing of Arlington, Massachusetts. No street address or phone number.

Naturally my daughter Amy and I were there when the electric cars came rolling into the Lake Morey Inn. Most of them looked like hot dogs on wheels. But, sure enough, the seventh vehicle to arrive looked like a regular car, except for its solar panels. I was thrilled. Amy and I pushed our way through the small crowd surrounding the car, and I explained to the youthful driver that I was in the market for just such a vehicle. Maybe we could sit down and discuss possibilities. He gave me an appalled look, and sped away.

"Talk to me in two years!" he called back.

As it turned out, Solectria began selling cars only sixteen months later, in September 1991. Too late for me. By then I was almost an old hand at EVs myself. Or at least an owner of some months' standing.

The event that excited me most at the symposium was the plenary session on Sunday morning. Four or five hundred of us heard a speech by a man named Roger Billings—a well-groomed and witty man in a dark blue business suit. He turned out to be a maker of fuel cells. He runs a research center in Missouri, somewhat confusingly called the American Academy of Science. The person who introduced him called him the leader in fuel-cell technology.

All right. What's a fuel cell? Among other things, it's a way of powering electric cars without using batteries. The kind Dr. Billings has developed consists of a metal box a little less than a foot square. Inside is a great deal of hydrogen—not as a compressed gas, but as a metallic hydrite. As this gasifies, it makes power. Enough, he claimed, to drive an electric car about nine times as far as Solo's batteries can. And also about twice as far as the average gasoline car. Five hundred miles on one charge. When you finally run out, you can recharge either of two ways. In about fifteen minutes at a special hydrogen charging station (if and when they exist). Or at home, overnight, plugged in—just as with batteries.

If that was all Dr. Billings had to say about fuel cells, I wouldn't have been so excited. There are always wild-eyed inventors around, telling anyone who will listen about their marvelous inventions. Some of them even wear dark blue business suits. And, alas, 99 percent of their inventions turn out not to work.

But fuel cells are already working, in places like the space shuttle. More to the point, there was already one working in an electric car—and Dr. Billings said he hoped to supply twenty prototype fuel cells to twenty more EVs during 1992. "If you're interested in getting one of them for your EV," he said to a very attentive audience, "we can probably supply you."

I am about as qualified to judge fuel cells as Calvin in the comic strip would be to judge the Ph.D. program at Stanford. Furthermore, I gathered that Billings is controversial in his field. That in no way diminished my optimism. I drove home from Boxborough on Sunday afternoon, thinking what if my next EV is powered by a fuel cell. One of the first things I'm going to do is drive to Boston on one charge, spend the night, get a taste of city life, and come back the next day still on that charge. If it weren't so damn far, I might also head out to Wendover, Utah, find that tall gas-pumper, and offer him a free tow for the gasoline vehicle of his choice.

CHAPTER 22

Solo Faces Winter

Only about two-fifths of the cranking power [of a car battery] available at 80° F is available when the temperature drops to 0° F.
—WALTER BILLIET, *Automotive Electrical Systems*

SOON AFTER I got back from Boxborough, Solo gave me my first bad scare. Daylight saving had just ended. Now it was going to be dark every night when I drove home. No harm in that—Solo can go a lot farther at night than I had dared to believe in Iowa City. It's just a little gloomier, commuting in the dark.

The first night turned out to be a *lot* gloomier. Seven miles from the college, my headlights began to dim. By the time I reached East Thetford, ten miles from the college, they weren't much better than a pair of flashlights. When I finally drove into my own barnyard, they had dwindled to two pools of moonlight.

Naturally I called Santa Rosa as soon as I got in the house and turned the lights on. Out there it was two-thirty on a sunny afternoon. I told Neil Sinclair what had happened. "I think the twelve-volt charger must not be working," I concluded.

"I think you're right," Neil readily agreed. "We've had two other people with the same problem. What it is, they've started making those little chargers too complicated. There's an extra chip that's supposed to keep your battery from overcharging. That's what fails."

"So, how do I get it fixed?"

"The simplest thing is to buy a new one," Neil said. "We get them from Sears here in Santa Rosa. You should be able to pick up one there. Be about thirty-five dollars."

"And then what?"

There was a long pause. "I think you probably better get someone to put it in for you," Neil said.

So here, just after the six-month mark, was my first real repair. If I had to have one, the timing couldn't have been better. The new ammeter was still lying on Solo's back seat. I could get whoever replaced the twelve-volt charger to install that at the same time.

And who would that be? Well, Dave Ring is going to be my long-term EV mechanic, I hope. He's the garage owner and tire dealer near White River Junction who is building his own electric car. But he has only just started. I decided to save him for later. Right now I'd use a college student. I was confident of getting a good one, because during the summer I had finally met Douglas Fraser. Doug is a research engineer at Dartmouth, and the driving force behind the college's annual entry in the Tour de Sol. Students build the car. Doug advises.

"Doug, I need a mechanic," I said. "Have you got a student who could do really first-class work on my car? I'd pay fifteen dollars an hour."

That may not sound like much to people who are used to seeing signs on garage walls say "Labor: $28 an hour" or "Labor: $36 an hour," but it sounds like a lot to most Dartmouth students. The ones who work as assistants in the college library start at $5.35 an hour.

The next day Darshan Bhatia called me. A senior, an enginnering major, a three-year veteran of electric car building, Darshan is from Hyderabad, India. Dartmouth usually has about fifty Indian students (and rather more Native Americans).

We quickly agreed that he would replace the charger, install the ammeter, and do a couple of little cosmetic things as well. He proceeded to do everything I wanted, spending ten hours in the process. When he had finished, he took me for a ride in his own car, a very small, very fast Italian sports car which can all but climb telephone poles.

"I thought you liked electric cars," I said, half-teasing.

"I do," Darshan answered. "But you know college students. We also like speed and noise. I think that in about five years I will be driving EVs for the rest of my life. I just want to have a little fun first." Darshan, meet world society.

I had plenty of money to pay Darshan, because after innumerable paperwork delays, I had finally sold the California truck. Got my $3,500, too. It doesn't really match John Fratcher's record with the moving van, because I had to put $50 in the radiator once I reached a cold climate and $165 into a new exhaust system before the truck could pass state inspection. Now if it had been an electric pickup . . .

The running ammeter has kept me busy and happy. From the moment Darshan brought Solo back to the moment I write his, I have been an eager dial-watcher. The most interesting thing I've learned is that you can trick an EV. Say you're going down from East Thetford to Hanover, along the Connecticut River. The road is fairly level. The speed limit is 50, and you're going about 52. You're drawing 150 amps. You tip your foot up from the accelerator for a second, and then put it very lightly down again. You continue going 52 mph, and now you're only drawing 90 amps. That may last for several miles. On a very slight downgrade, I once cruised at 60 mph, drawing only 50 amps.

The new ammeter has also enabled me to do some systematic testing of what happens on hills. Naturally I did the tests on Thetford Hill, using both sides. Sometimes I drove up the east side—a comparatively gradual two-mile climb, coming up from the river, past the high terrace where the good farms are, up to the village of Thetford Hill, perched on top of the ridge. Sometimes I drove up the west side—the shorter, steeper climb up from my own village. On each side I have experimented with first, second, third, and fourth gears. Fifth is out of the question.

Obviously I wasn't born to be a test driver, because I could seldom get the same results twice. A lot remains unclear. I am certain of this much, though. Solo would use the least power if I always took him up in first. He can go all the way up the steeper side in first gear using just 100 amps—and that result *was* consistent over three tries.

I have no plans, however, ever to take him up in first again.

Between his panels and the lettering on his back and sides, Solo is pretty clearly an electric car. I would be making enemies for the EV movement every trip. In first gear Solo goes up at a steady 15 mph. Even some trucks do better than that.

Second is faster, but not much. Using 150 amps, I could start up at 25 mph. But unless I fed it more amps, the car soon slowed to 20, and crawled steadily to the top at that speed.

The way I normally go up is either in third or fourth. Fourth if I have a running start, third if I don't. In both gears I am going to use 280 or 300 or even 350 amps. Third gear seems to work best. I go up at a steady 33 mph, usually drawing just over 300 amps. Even that speed doesn't delight cars that sometimes swoop up behind me— but Thetford's elementary school, fire department, and oldest church are right at the top, and they're going to have to slow down to 30, anyway. On the hill itself the speed limit is 40. I don't feel excessively guilty.

Soon it was the middle of November, and getting cold. One morning when the temperature was about fifteen, I tried the heater. Not because my hands were cold—I had gloves on. I was just curious to see how the heater worked. Adequately. It will take frost stars off the windshield. But I do not like it. It makes a frantic little noise, which I suppose is meant to fool you into thinking it must be pouring streams of hot air out. It isn't.

Then it got to be December, and truly cold weather came slamming in. On December 5 the temperature was zero when Anne and I woke up, and not more than five above when I left for work and she for Barnet. In the first couple of miles, Solo demonstrated one of his advantages over gas cars. On a zero morning, a combustion engine does not combust well for some time. It is hard to start, feeble when you do get it started. Pathetic on a hill. But Solo, fat and saucy from the photovoltaics on my barn, started out at full vigor. So what if I am drawing 300 amps as I glide up Thetford Hill at my usual 33 mph? I can plug in at the college, and plan to. I know about batteries and cold weather.

Probably if I had stayed in Hanover all day, there would have been no problem. But I was there only three hours: just long enough to go to a department meeting, talk with an honors student, and have a quick lunch with a friend. Solo therefore got to charge for only three hours. Even then, if the voltage in Murdough were as high as in most college buildings, I'd have been all right. But it isn't—not that I knew that on December 5. What I knew was that for some curious reason whenever I plugged in behind Murdough, Solo began to charge at only 6 amps. It had hitherto been enough.

It wasn't today. I started home. Got to East Thetford with ease. Then halfway up Thetford Hill from the river, Solo gave an almost audible sigh, and began to slow down. Three-quarters of the way up, I faced reality and pulled over. At least a dozen gasoline cars passed me during the ten minutes I sat there, waiting for the batteries to repolarize. Of course, I imagined each driver grinning, and drawing conclusions about electric cars that would be partly erroneous and partly correct.

When Buildings and Grounds sent an electrician to meet me at Murdough two days later, he quickly found the problem. The building's voltage is only 110. Next door, at the Thayer School of Engineering, they have 115. When we plugged Solo in at their loading dock as a test, he instantly and gratefully began to draw 11 amps. But the college can't let me park in front of the Thayer School's loading dock all winter; it would annoy all the trucks making deliveries. There seems to be no other outside circuit anywhere near my office. The result was delightful. I didn't have to wait for spring to get my reserved parking place in a regular lot. I got it in December, and even on very cold days I can count on 11 or 12 amperes. So far the college has not billed me for my half of the cost of installing the outlet.

On January 6, 1992, Environmental Studies 1 had its first class meeting at 10:00 A.M. There were fifty students present, and a professor. This year, as in 1990, the first book in the course was John McPhee's *Encounters with the Archdruid*. The professor did not know whether he would be able to resist making wisecracks about David Brower and the need for a mule. He did know that if a student raised her hand, and started asking questions about his own travel habits, he at last had an adequate answer ready.

CHAPTER 23

Death of an Electric Car

The useful life of an electric vehicle [is] anywhere from
25 percent to 100 percent longer than the correspond-
ing life of a combustion vehicle.
—ANDREW FORD, *The Impact of Electric Vehicles on
the Southern California Edison System,* 1992

SOLO GOT THROUGH the winter nicely. I always plugged in at
work, and I always drove home without incident. Since I was
now in my office five days a week, and occasionally on a Saturday or Sunday as well, I averaged 200 miles a week. In the gas-
guzzling farm pickup (which I still owned) that would have taken
just under ten gallons of gasoline. In Solo it took the full production
of my solar panels, plus a little bit of electricity from the power company. Nothing else.

I got almost a miser's pleasure, as the term rolled along, in thinking of all the gasoline I hadn't burned. By the sixth week I had not
used a full barrel, and by the end of the term I had not used two bar-
rels. That's three times my own weight in gasoline that I hadn't consumed. (The average American driver, in case you're wondering,
burns about twenty times his or her weight in gasoline every year.)

I did employ the guzzler to go up to my wife's house now and
then. But since this winter I was teaching and she wasn't, mostly she
came down to my house—and stayed good stretches at a time.

The one time Solo embarrassed me was during the last week of classes. Long past McPhee now, past the journals of Lewis and Clark, past Edward Abbey's *Desert Solitaire*, we were ending the course with a science fiction novel called *Penterra*. It takes place in the year 2233, at which time the planet is rather a mess. I happen to know the author, a woman named Judith Moffett. She had agreed to come up to Dartmouth to teach one of the classes on her book, so that students could meet a live author, and could also ask if she really believed the earth was going to be like that in two hundred years. (She does.)

Judy arrived on the kind of warm March day we occasionally get. I met her at the airport in Solo, and she enjoyed her first ride in an EV. But the next day was back to normal March weather in Vermont—cold, and snow blowing about. Solo's little heater does fine in southern California, less well here. About a quarter of the way in to the college, Judy's teeth began to chatter.

"I wish I'd brought longjohns," she said wistfully. From that she went on to wish out loud for fur-lined gloves, more scarves, a snowmobile suit, and finally a different vehicle. It was clear to me that whatever else was wrong in 2233, the EVs, electric helicopters, etc., then in use had excellent heating systems. As, indeed, EVs are starting to right now—and without the use of propane. You'll see.

Apart from that one chill-out, Solo went on to do nicely in the spring, summer, and fall of 1992. Not just in driving, but in endurance. His batteries showed no signs of aging. As I seldom ran the charge down below half, I began to think they might go not only three years, but well beyond.

But on December 28, 1992, Solo abruptly died. I was zipping along a two-lane highway, one of the straightest and most nearly level roads in this whole region. A few miles north of Hanover, I began to close in rapidly on a gravel truck. Loaded to the gills, it was just crawling along.

I could see half a mile ahead. Nothing coming. I swung out to pass. But just as I drew abreast, I realized that this big square truck was in the process of turning left. Hadn't the driver signaled? I now believe he had. But the signal lights on a gravel truck tend to be dusty or muddy or both. I had seen no flashing red lights.

I had some fraction of a second to make a choice. I could try to shoot past before he completed the turn. Or I could try to turn even further left than he was, and escape out into the hayfield that ran along the side of the road. My hands, not my brain, opted for the swing left.

For another fraction of a second, the plan seemed to work. Solo shot in front of the truck, just brushing its left front tire. Then he and I slammed into a phone pole. We were going fifty-five miles an hour.

Not only did I live, I wasn't even bleeding when I struggled out the half-crumpled door on the passenger side. The car wasn't bleeding, either. There was a monster dent in front, exactly the size and shape of a telephone pole, but there was no flood of sulfuric acid from the forward batteries. No hiss of steam from the radiator. (Couldn't be. No radiator.) Dazed as I felt, I still was able to notice the one tiny bit of silver lining. This head-on crash showed that electric cars are pretty safe in accidents, maybe safer than gasoline cars. At least Solo was.

Ten minutes later the ambulance arrived, and I was on my way to the hospital. They let me go home again that night.

But though Solo had done such a good job of protecting me— my only serious injury was a cracked collarbone, caused by the seat belt that helped to save my life—and though he had not sprung a leak or burst into flames or anything, he himself was damaged beyond repair. Even I could see how badly the frame was sprung.

What, if you live in rural Vermont, do you do with the corpse of an electric car? A year earlier, the answer would have been: not much. The engineering students at Dartmouth knew lots about solar racing cars, but they hadn't the time, the tools, or even the workspace to deal with full-size EVs. In the fall of 1991, when I hired Darshan to install the new ammeter, he had had to do the work in a chilly parking lot. Dave Ring, the owner of Tip Top Tire, was still planning to build an EV, but still hadn't got started.

But someone else had. By the winter of 1992, change was beginning to come fast in the electric car world. Instead of the three little companies that existed when I bought Solo, now there were at least fifteen. One of them was called Vermont Electric Cars. The three young men who owned it (and were the entire workforce) had their shop just outside Montpelier, the very small city that is Vermont's capital. Naturally I had come to know them. In fact, they had just finished making me a couple of high-tech charging cords that worked much better on rainy days than the ordinary orange cords you pick up in a hardware store.

I called the one I knew best, a man named Steve Miracle. That's his real name, and a very good one it is for someone in the EV business. By now several days had passed. I had my left arm in a sling, and many interesting shades of purple and yellow could be seen in the vicinity of my eyes, but I was functional.

"Steve, I'm going to need you to make me a new electric car," I said.

"Yeah, I heard about Solo," he answered. "A shame."

"I'm hoping you can reuse a good many of his parts."

"Can't tell until we look. But it sounds as if we could use the PV panels and the tires for sure. Probably we can salvage the motor and the main charger, too. Maybe even the controller."

"Good."

"Though, you know," he added, "there are a couple of new controllers out, a lot better than the one you've got. And not too expensive, either. Might be worth getting."

"If they're better, let's get one. How soon can you start?" I asked, patient as usual.

"Well, we've got a car we just started, for a lady down near Bennington. The first one we'll be selling, actually. It'll be a while."

"How much of a while?"

"We could probably start in the spring."

My wife had been listening to my end of this conversation. "I want an electric car, too," she told me as soon as I had relayed Steve's end. "Especially," she said thoughtfully, "if it can have regen braking. I want to be able to get from my house to yours, and not worry. Tell Steve to save all of Solo that's savable for my car, and you get yourself a replacement for him right now." She laughed. "Your course starts next week, and you *know* there's going to be at least one Alison in it."

"You're a darling," I said.

So I began thinking both where to get a new EV right now, and how to pay for it. The money—most of it, anyway—I expected to get from my insurance. Complete with panels, Solo had cost $17,500, and he was only twenty months old. Considering the long life span of EVs, surely he was still worth something like two-thirds of his purchase price.

As for the replacement, well, there were a lot of choices. One that I did not even consider was heading back to Santa Rosa. I had stayed in touch with Dick Frost and Gary Starr at Solar Electric, which is now called Electricar. I knew the company was booming. Really booming. I could get one of Solo's young brothers or sisters, and it would be a much improved model, a car I'd be happy to own. But it would not be a car—not yet—that I'd be happy to drive home from California.

Mind you, I do still plan another cross-country EV trip. Plans, however, call for it to be an easy, casual, offhand success. I want to drive my 100 or 150 miles, charge up quickly and conveniently, and then drive some more. I want filling-station attendants to look with admiration and envy.

Already these desires are more plausible than they would have been in 1991. As to range: Several types of improved batteries are nearing the market right now. You'll hear more about them later. As to ease of charging: In the last three years probably a thousand public charging stations have been opened in the United States. There are several hundred new ones in California alone. There are twenty stations either already built or in the process of being built right here in little Vermont. One even uses photovoltaics. Among the customers are the nine electric vehicles the state has recently acquired.

But even after all this progress, I still would not feel comfortable setting out to cross Nevada by EV. Nor climbing Donner Pass. You could certainly do both of those things in one of the super-EVs that weigh only half as much as ordinary cars and that carry $25,000 worth of high-tech batteries. Several people have. But super-EVs are out of my price range.

In fact, as I've said, *any* new car, EV or guzzler, was out of my price range until I got the insurance money for Solo. This, I assumed, would be within a week or two. The company would just have to satisfy itself that Solo was truly totaled, and then it would send a large check. Routine stuff. Auto insurance companies pay for thousands of accidents every day. And I was with an outstandingly efficient company called AMICA.

I nevertheless got no check within a week or two. It took the whole rest of the winter to settle the case. Meanwhile, I commuted to class in the farm pickup—and kept my mouth tightly shut about David Brower and his need for a mule.

Paying me took AMICA so long for a very good reason. There were simply no precedents. AMICA had never dealt with an electric car accident before. Or if they had, it was so long ago—back in the first heyday of EVs, before World War One—that not even the oldest adjuster remembered a thing about it. And there was another problem, too. My car had a dual personality.

Solo, you'll recall, began life as a 1985 Ford Escort station wagon, and ran around for six years emitting fumes. Then, still keeping his original vehicle identification number, he got born again. Now he was what Solar Electric called an Electron One. These two identities were merged in my insurance policy, where he was described as an Electron One Ford Escort.

The very junior adjuster who received my accident report concentrated on the last two words. First he confirmed that Solo was totaled. Then he looked up the book value of ordinary 1985 Ford Escort station wagons, and found it to be $1,700. Then he did a little subtraction. To keep the premium down, my collision insurance has a $500 deductible. So he deducted it. "We'll be sending you a check for $1,200," he told me over the phone. AMICA, he added, would simultaneously take title to what was left of Solo.

Naturally I protested, and the young adjuster was not adamant. He heard my case on how much more Solo had been worth before the accident, and my other case on how useful the carcass would be to me, and how useless to AMICA.

A few days later he called back with a revised offer. On the book value he was unshakable. The book simply didn't mention Electron

Ones (or Electricar, for that matter), but it had plenty to say about Ford Escorts. "We can allow $1,200," he repeated.

But then he came to his two concessions, and they were real ones. "We're agreeable to your keeping the six solar panels at no cost," he said. And then, after I had removed them, they were prepared to sell me back Solo's ruined body for only $150.

I am generally grateful for concessions, but this second one underwhelmed me. One effect would be to cut my little check down to $1,050. That works out to 6.8 percent of the original purchase price. Not even enough for a down payment on a new car.

Not that I could have bought a new EV on time, anyway. In January of 1993 there was no company prepared to sell an EV on time. Electricar has since begun to, but it didn't then. It and most of the other small companies in the EV business wanted money up front, before they even started work on the car. Just as I'd had to pay an advance on Solo.

So I rejected the young adjuster's second offer. Then I wrote an eloquent letter to AMICA's headquarters in Rhode Island, saying just what you'd expect me to say about the cost and value of electric cars, and about the company's chance to help in bringing about a low-pollution future.

The result was prompt and wonderful. A senior adjuster named Dick Lein took over the case. He proceeded to shatter any preconceptions I may have had about officials in the insurance industry, such as that they tend to pettifog, or that they measure their success by how little they pay out.

Since the first page of the book that will give the book value of EVs has yet to be written, what Dick did was to talk to electric car converters around the country. A couple of the names he got from me; the others he found himself. I think he even located what was at that time the only used EV dealer in the United States. Then he called me back with a question. "What would you say your car was worth at the time of the crash?" he asked casually. "Minus, of course, the solar panels, which, as you know, we are prepared to give you."

"It was only twenty months old," I answered. "I think it was worth $10,000."

"That's a little higher than what I've heard," Dick said agreeably. "But it's in the ballpark. I've heard eight or nine thousand mostly, though there's one fellow in California who would go higher. I was thinking of eight. You want ten. Let's split the difference. We'll pay you nine. And you can keep the wreck."

CHAPTER 24

The Electric Luxury Car

Reporter: Do you find that electric car owners have much in common besides interest in their automobiles?

Dr. Robert Zickefoose, Senior Engineering Project Manager, Alternative Energy Corporation: They do. They are generally concerned about the environment, and actually trying to do something themselves to improve it. You might think they would be tinkerers or mechanically inclined individuals, but I don't find this to be the case.
—RALEIGH REPORTER, *June 6, 1993*

I T WAS NOW EARLY March. With $9,000 in my pocket and a considerable list of EV companies in my head, I was ready to go find a new car. A few months earlier, I would probably have looked first at the Impact. I'd had a chance to drive one at an electric auto show in Boston, and I'd liked it a lot. The design was a little racy for my sober tastes, but the acceleration matched that of most sports cars, and the regenerative braking worked like a dream.

General Motors still wasn't saying when the car would go into production, but in the fall of 1992 car magazines were full of what seemed to be well-informed rumors. One rumor repeated what I'd already heard. GM would do an initial run in 1993. Then it provided details. The company would start modestly, building 5,000 electric cars the first year. And a truly delicious piece of new (rumored) information: Impacts would probably sell for $17,000.

Not bad. My insurance check would cover only a little over half of that—but Americans have a way of finding extra money when they're out buying cars. Besides, I no longer believed that solar panels were much use on heavy commuter vehicles, and I could raise part of the cost by selling the six that had been on Solo. They're plenty of use on houses.

But there were no Impacts to look at. Not in March 1993. A new board had taken over at GM, and one of its first actions had been to cancel plans for the production and sale of EVs. Well, not actually cancel, but postpone for at least four years. There were rumors about that, too. A couple of engineers from GM's electric car program had said they believed production had been put off not because the board didn't think the car would sell, but because they feared it would. That was pure paranoia, perhaps. And perhaps not. GM has subverted electric transportation before. Most famously, the company bought up many trolley lines in the 1930s and then closed them down, so as to create a bigger market for gasoline buses. GM eventually got taken to court, was convicted, and was fined a token sum.

That's ancient history, though, and certainly not to be blamed on the company's present management. To me, the real irony lies in something quite contemporary. At almost the same moment that GM canceled 1993 production of the Impact, Honda also announced a cancellation. Only theirs was of the Honda racing team. The roughly hundred engineers involved were transferred to the Honda electric car program.

GM didn't back out altogether. About the middle of 1993 the company announced that it would still carry out 1 percent of the original plan. That is, it would make fifty Impacts. None would be for sale. Thirty would be used in a series of elaborate consumer trials over a period of two years. The other twenty would mostly go to power companies, for fleet testing. One GM spokesman commented that if they *were* for sale, they ought to cost at least $25,000.

You think that's high? About the same time, Edward Hagenlocker, executive vice-president of Ford, offered a truly breathtaking figure. "We can build an electric car that the American customer would want, but it will cost him $100,000." Another GM official said that he personally didn't think the American customer wanted EVs at any price. I could have told him otherwise. I have friends in GM's electric car program, and I know they have already gotten thousands of attempted orders, some accompanied by would-be cash deposits. I guess in a company as big as GM, it's not just that the left hand doesn't always know what the right hand is doing. The company is more like the Hindu goddess Kali, who has rows of hands. Hand Three may be directly counteracting Hand One, while Hand Four ignores them both.

But never mind GM. Never mind Ford, which has made a few electric Ecostars that it rents to power companies—at a cool $40,000 a year. Never mind Chrysler, which has made a few electric vans that it has sold, also to power companies, for the awesome price of $120,000 each. (Late in 1993 they did cut the price, but hardly to bargain level. As I write, Chrysler electric vans cost one hagen-locker, or precisely $100,000.) Why would power companies buy at either price? Because it's very much in their interest to encourage the development of EVs.

But me, I had other choices. For example, Solar Car, down in Florida, was thriving—and had just been invited by the state of Connecticut to open a branch plant up there. It would build both electric cars and electric buses. This Connecticut plant wouldn't open anywhere near in time for me, but no matter. The East Coast is level, and it is well supplied with electrical outlets. If I wanted to, I could take my guzzling pickup down there, and for $14,000 bring it home as an EV.

And if I didn't want to, I could just hop down to Massachusetts. Solectria, conveniently near Boston, now had its high-tech little electric Geos in production—and had recently sold ten of them to Boston Edison. They were quite ready to sell me one for $26,000.

These prices, though a tiny fraction of Chrysler's or Ford's, were still much higher than the cost of comparable gasoline cars, not to mention than the $9,000 I had received from AMICA. Well, I had some other sources in mind, too. Also handily in Massachusetts is a company called Electric Vehicles of America. They'd do me a pickup conversion for $13,000. Scattered around the United States, I knew of a dozen other small companies that were prepared to sell me an EV. They ranged from the wholly inaccessible, like Beetles Unlimited of Seattle (an electric VW for $15,500), to the merely inconvenient, like BAT International of Utah (a converted Geo Metro for $15,900). By "inaccessible" I only mean: a long way from Vermont.

I also knew about one actual dealer, Green Motorworks of North Hollywood, California. Green Motorworks carries several different makes of EVs, including one import. That's the little Danish car called the Kewet. It sells for $12,900. Unlike most current EVs, Kewets are built from scratch as electrics, and have the advantage of light weight. They don't go fast enough for my taste, but they must be exceptionally tough. At any rate, a young German named Robert Mohr is driving one around the world. The last I heard, he had gone through Austria, Hungary, most of the former Soviet Union, Japan, Australia, and was headed from Los Angeles down to Brazil.

Curiously enough, the U.S. section was in some ways the hardest part of his trip. That's because 99 percent of the electrical outlets in this country are 110 volt, which from the point of view of an EV owner is low. Plug your car in, and you get to wait eight hours while it charges. Most countries handle this better. They run on 220 volts, and an electric car can have a full meal in three hours. That made the trip easier for Mohr. He could drive his Kewet 50 or 60 miles, stop for three hours, drive, stop for three hours, drive again. He generally did 150 and often 180 miles a day. He did not attempt either Donner Pass or Nevada.

Kewets are nice. So are Solar Car's Fords and Solectria's little Geos, and I like the sound of those Beetles. But as it turned out I didn't choose any of the vehicles I've been talking about.

At the same EV show where I'd driven an Impact, I had gotten to know Bob Batson, the owner of the company called Electric Vehicles of America. Besides doing conversions, Bob also runs one of the few EV service stations in the East. Besides all that, he has been the consultant to numerous schools, colleges, and individuals who were thinking EV. He now became my consultant, too.

Bob knew I was no tinkerer, not mechanically inclined. He didn't even try to interest me in a conversion kit. He also knew the size of my Solo check, and decided to find me a car to match.

"Noel," he called me one day to ask, "can you manage $10,000? If so, I've got a car for you. It's an electric Audi, converted last year."

An Audi! I have spent my whole life owning Chevy pickups and Toyota pickups and humble Plymouth coupes, plus of course one Ford Escort turned electric. Luxury cars were to me a field unknown.

"Who? Where? How?" I asked.

Answering my questions in turn, Bob said the Audi belonged to a young computer engineer named Larry Cassese, who had done the conversion in 1992. The car could be seen right there in the Boston suburbs, where Larry lived. He was selling it because he (a tinkerer) had had such fun building it that now he wanted to do another. First he needed to get his money back out of this one. Bob Batson had been his consultant right along. Both men were members of the New England chapter of the Electric Auto Association.

Soon thereafter I had Larry on the phone, and a few days later my wife and I were in Wayland, Massachusetts, staring at an electric Audi.

What we saw in the Casseses' driveway was a handsome gray four-door sedan. It was well along in years—a 1983 model—but it gleamed like new. Audi must know a lot about high-class paint.

Soon we were taking a test drive. What's more, we were taking it in comfortable warmth. It was a cold March day, but the electric heater Larry had installed coped easily.

This was none of your round-the-block test drives. We went almost thirty miles. Larry drove the outward bound section; Anne and I divided the trip home. Only one thing disappointed me. I salivate when I think of regenerative braking, and this car didn't have it. Oh well, my third EV will.

Everything else we liked a lot. I finally learned what makers of luxury cars mean when they boast about the car's "ride"; this Audi gave you the sort of feeling you get when you're a small child and you climb into your grandmother's lap. More important, it had a good range. I'd just seen it go twenty-nine miles on half a charge. It was easy to believe Larry when he said he did his forty-mile round-trip commute with no trouble, except on a few zero days in winter. Those few days he needed to plug in at work. It was just my experience with Solo, except that there are a lot more zero days in Vermont, and my daily round trip is only twenty-seven (somewhat more hilly) miles.

Another thing that pleased me was the instrument panel. I especially liked the fuel gauge, which I'd naturally looked at a good many times during the test drive. It resembled Solo's in consisting of ten light-up bars, but it was a different and better make. Solo's gauge was a crazy optimist, still reporting a quarter of a charge when the batteries were actually almost drained. The Audi's gauge I would call a cautious realist. The first couple of bars drop rather fast, and from then on each bar lasts longer and longer. When the gauge reports a quarter of a charge, you have 30 percent.

When we got back to Wayland, Larry opened the hood and trunk, and I pretended to study the motor and battery set-up. Anne sensibly went in the house with Alison Cassese. It was cold.

I may not be mechanically clever, but I can count. There were only sixteen batteries in the main pack, as opposed to Solo's seventeen. So how did this car manage to have better range? Then I realized they were larger batteries: T-145s instead of T-125s. As near as I could figure, the net effect (if the cars were equal in all other respects) would be to give the Audi a 9 percent better range than Solo's. Nowhere near enough to impress Edward Hagenlocker, but valuable to me.

By now I was ready to buy. Larry, however, was not ready to sell. Why? He wasn't sure I knew the car's faults well enough yet. He is one of the most scrupulously honest people I have ever met. In preparation for our visit, he had written out a list of the Audi's defects (his word), and this he now wanted to go over with me.

There were four items on the list. One of them Anne and I already knew about from the test drive: Two of the four door handles on this car didn't work right. One rear door was difficult to open from the outside, and the other was impossible. You had to grope around inside, and open it that way. The other defects consisted of a one-inch crack in the trim on the front bumper, a loose wire in the horn, and a periodic problem with something called the DC-to-DC converter. This handy device eliminates the need for a separate charger for the 12-volt battery. Whenever you're driving, the DC-to-DC converter takes a little power from the main battery pack and uses it to keep the 12-volt battery primed. Larry had been having some trouble keeping it grounded properly.

"I really don't want to sell you the car until I get that fixed," he said. "Bob tells me you're a literature teacher. Give me another week."

Scrupulousness breeds scrupulousness. "Okay," I agreed, "but I reserve the right to pay for the hours you put in working on it."

There were ten such hours. So in the end I bought the car for $10,250. And because I was still busily teaching Environmental Studies 1 and having end-of-term conferences, I made no effort to bring the car home myself. About that time, Robert Mohr was driving his Kewet across Russia. I had my Audi trucked to Vermont.

Spring, summer, and fall passed as uneventfully with the Audi as they had the previous year with Solo. I took advantage of the 9 percent increase in range (it's actually turned out to be more like 15 percent) to begin driving up to my wife's house in warm weather, and thus not to use another barrel or two of gasoline. I gave the car a name, and not a very original one. For years I had smiled at what I had seen as the pretentiousness of boat owners who keep using the same name over and over, so that you see Mary Lou III or Sea Sprite IV painted on the stern of a sailboat. But now I understand that it needn't be vanity, just some mix of loyalty, love, and habit. Somehow the Audi became Solo. When necessary, Solo II. At least it's not painted on the trunk.

The farthest I drove Solo II on one charge that summer was fifty-four miles. You are not impressed? You remember that Solo I went sixty and sixty-one miles as he crossed through Illinois and Indiana? Ah, but he didn't go sixty-one miles in Vermont or New Hampshire. Someone has calculated that driving in northern New England is like continuously going up a 2 percent grade, climbing a gentle hill forever. Naturally you pay in energy. It takes half again as much power to go up a 2 percent grade as it does to drive on the level. If I lived in Illinois, I think I could get a summer range of eighty miles.

The spring of 1993 was not only a good time for Solo II, it was a good time for electric cars in the whole region. Parking, for example, improved dramatically. I had long had a promise from the town manager of Hanover that when there were three EVs in town, he'd install a charging station.

But now the manager, a scholarly-looking man named Cliff Vermilya, decided not to wait. First he picked a spot in the most desirable downtown parking lot. Then he got Granite State Electric to wire up a double charging facility—one outlet for the reserved EV parking place, and another for possible future expansion. For now, the electricity would be free, a gift of the taxpayers. (Don't forget they are getting avoided pollution costs in return.) Finally, Cliff had a large sign put up, which threatens any gasoline car presuming to use the EV space with a $55 fine.

As I write, Solo II is still the only electric vehicle in Hanover. But he is about to have company. At this very minute an electric pickup is being built for the Hanover police department. This is just the meter truck. But Chief Schimke is already dreaming of the day, a few years from now, when he can order the first electric cruiser.

Nor will the count stop at two. Plans are afoot for a second electric pickup, probably to be owned by the Thayer School of Engineering. After that, the next likely target is the medical center, and then the local airport. (Ground vehicles at airports are among the biggest polluters in the United States, and a drive is just beginning to make most of them electric. The first electric shuttle buses have already arrived at Los Angeles International Airport.)

Another spring event took place in the Vermont legislature. A bill finally passed which makes the registration fee for EVs the same as that for gasoline vehicles. Am I responsible? No. The zeitgeist is. It did get a lot of help, to be sure, from State Representative Doris Lingelbach of Thetford and State Senator Stephen Webster of Orange County. Obviously they didn't go to all that trouble for one voter; they were acting, if I may put it a little grandiosely, for the planet.

Summer went well, too. On July 1, something really nice happened for potential EV-owners all over the country. A new federal law came into effect. What it says is that you can take 10 percent of the cost of an EV off your income tax. If I had waited until July to buy the Audi, I could have knocked $1,025 off my 1992 income tax. (Why didn't I wait? Didn't hear about the new law in time.) If you bought a new Solectria tomorrow, you could save $2,605 on your income tax. And so on. The one thing you couldn't do is buy a Big Three EV for $100,000, and take $10,000 off. The government, perhaps agreeing with me that current EV prices in Detroit are ridiculous, has limited the maximum tax saving per vehicle to $4,000.

Slightly later in the summer came another step forward for Vermont. The Pentagon has a new rule, as surprising as it is wonderful, that it can't spend quite all its money on weapons. A little bit has to go to post–Cold War civilian technology. And in the summer of 1993, a little bit of that little bit came to Vermont. To be precise, the state got a quarter of a million. Militarily, $250,000 might buy a few inches on one wing of a warplane. But now it was going to yield the nine EVs I have already mentioned, plus the twenty charging stations, plus a lot of testing. To be sure, these Pentagon grants require matching money. That quickly came in the form of $50,000 each from several power companies, and smaller amounts from numerous sources, including New England Telephone and Ben and Jerry's ice cream. But the total for everything is only $610,000. Maybe a foot on one wing? Instead, four electric pickups, two electric cars, two electric vans, and one EV pickup with four-wheel drive.

My wife's electric car has been delayed, because she's been sick. But there are still getting to be a respectable number of EVs in the state, as there are in most states. The time is already here when I could take the whole Environmental Studies 1 class on a field trip, traveling in an electric caravan. When you consider that in January 1990 I couldn't even find one lone EV for myself, and that it took me the whole next year *to* find one, it seems like considerable progress.

CHAPTER 25

Electric Cars
Face the Future

The once-despised electric has amply proved its usefulness. Its sun is rising, not setting.
—HERBERT TOWLE, "Electric Vehicles—Today and Tomorrow," *Collier's,* January 7, 1911

THERE IS NOT much question that electric cars face a bright future. Every major automobile company in the world is either making one or getting ready to make one. Almost every government in the industrialized world is providing incentives for this to happen. Germany, for example, recently exempted EV-owners from user taxes for a period of five years. The French government is deeply involved with a plan to introduce EVs in twenty-two French cities, each of which will have both standard and special rapid (i.e., high voltage) charging stations. One of the twenty-two cities, La Rochelle, has already received its first fifty electric cars, and they are currently available for rent at public parking lots.

In Switzerland, there are already a couple of thousand EVs on the road. They're mostly for city use, not for climbing the Alps. And they are highly affordable. I've seen published reports that in Switzerland an electric "sells for less than an average small car." (Hear that, Ford? Want to check that out, Chrysler?) One reason for the good price, though hardly the only one, is that most cantons forgo the purchase tax that conventional cars must pay. The Swiss purchaser of an EV saves somewhere between $350 and $550.

Glance at East Asia. Japan's Ministry of International Trade and Industry is pressing hard to get 200,000 EVs on Japanese roads by the end of the decade. With government backing, a company in Taiwan has begun production of a tiny EV that sells for under $5,000. The Korean government says it is determined to make Korea the world leader in EVs by the end of the decade. And so on.

Here at home, not only the federal government but around twenty of the states offer various inducements to makers and buyers of EVs, and four have flat-out requirements.

By far the best known is California's requirement that first 2 percent, then 5 percent, then 10 percent of all new cars sold there be zero-emission. That is to say, electric. Rod and I were arguing about that in Wyoming. The rule takes effect in 1998; 2 percent begins that year.

Less well known is the fact that New York, Massachusetts, and Maine have all adopted the same rule. Several other states, such as Maryland and New Jersey, have said that if and when all bordering states adopt the rule, they'll automatically join in. Fourteen more states are seriously considering the 2-5-10 requirement. If, as seems likely, most of them do join in, there will be an assured EV market that starts in 1998 at about 80,000 electric cars a year. Over the next five years, the market will grow to 400,000 EVs annually.

Who will buy all these cars? Some will go to utility companies and to state and federal agencies, many of which are required to convert part of their fleets to electric or natural gas or both. Most, of course, will go to private citizens, people looking for a new car and deciding on an electric, just as you'd decide on a Buick or a Saab.

What if there aren't 80,000 car-buyers in 1998 who want an electric? Or 400,000 electric enthusiasts in 2003? Will people be compelled to buy them? Will dealers hold lotteries, and the loser gets an EV? Will state motor vehicle bureaus have computer programs that flag every tenth would-be registrant? And order him or her to go buy an electric?

No. Nothing like that will happen. The California–New York–Maine–Massachusetts rules do not require one single person to buy an EV. They merely require the big auto companies, domestic and foreign, to sell them. "Sell" means not just offering them for sale, but actually talking customers—first 2 percent, then 5 percent, then 10 percent—into buying them.

The law does allow some flexibility. It also offers rewards. Suppose GM has to sell 6,000 EVs in California in 1998, which is about what I think they will have to—but actually does sell 8,204. The company could make a tidy extra profit by selling credit for the surplus to another manufacturer. Or suppose, still needing to sell 6,000, GM continues to think small, and only gets around to building and selling 50. They'll have to buy credits like crazy.

Naturally these rules make the Big Three (not to mention the Formidable Five, or whatever the big Japanese companies call themselves) extremely nervous. The current line in Detroit is that any EV that customers will actually want to buy will cost—not Mr. Hagenlocker's absurd $100,000, but $5,000 to $10,000 more than a comparable gasoline car.

And why, thinks Detroit, will anyone pay $5,000 or $10,000 more for a car that has a shorter range and takes a long time to refuel? They won't, thinks Detroit. Therefore we auto manufacturers have two choices. We can lower the price of EVs artificially, and thus lose money on every one we sell. Or we can try to overturn the rules that make us sell them at all.

Actually, true to Kali of the many hands, the auto companies are working with both ideas simultaneously, plus several more. One thought is to lower the price of EVs but not lose money, because you simultaneously raise the price of gasoline cars in those states that require the EVs. How much? The math is simple. If 98 percent of the cars sold in New York, California, etc., in 1998 have combustion engines and 2 percent use electricity, and if the EVs cost $5,000 to $10,000 more, then a price hike of $200 per combustion car will do it nicely.

The figure will grow, of course. By 2003, when 10 percent of the new cars sold in California, etc., must be EVs, the buyers of combustion cars would be paying an extra $1,000. Even the mere prospect of this will naturally infuriate them, which I suspect is part of the plan. Why should they subsidize us EV-owners, they'll think. If we want to go around saving the planet, do it on our own money.

Don't worry; it won't be that way. I hope to show presently that *we'll* wind up subsidizing *them*.

The manufacturers are also busy thinking of ways to avoid the requirements altogether. The American Automobile Manufacturers Association has already brought suit in federal district courts, trying to keep New York, Massachusetts, and Maine from adopting the 2-5-10 requirement. California they have not brought suit against, because California's rule enjoys special status as something already in place before the amended Clean Air Act. But emissaries from Ford are lobbying hard for repeal, and highly reliable rumors say that the Automobile Manufacturers Association is planning an all-out attack both in California and in Washington, D.C. The main argument will be that EVs are just not practical.

They are practical, of course. As they move into mass production, they will get even more so. I mean, their prices will wind up at or below those of comparable gasoline cars, not just in Switzerland but everywhere. As batteries and hence driving ranges improve (and perhaps as hybrids come on the market), EVs will move from being commuter cars to all-purpose vehicles, perfectly suitable as the one car of a one-car family. In due time they'll even right the balance of trade.

But I was talking about state requirements and inducements. California is the prime requirer. Arizona, I think, is the prime inducer. Since the fall of 1991, Arizona has been offering EV-owners a deal that even Germans would respect.

Arizona is one of the states where you pay a huge sum to register a new car, a little less the next year, still less the third year, and so on.

Suppose you went to Phoenix tomorrow and bought a $20,000 gasoline car. To register it, you would pay the state fees totaling $489.75. Now suppose that instead you bought a $39,000 EV, maybe one of the spiffy Electricars that are in fact available in Phoenix. (And for 10 percent off, too, because of the federal tax credit.) For the Electricar you would pay fees totaling $25.35.

Next year you would pay $401 to register your now slightly used gasoline car, but only $23 for the Electricar. And so on, year after year. It could be many years, since EVs have a life expectancy about 50 percent longer than that of combustion-engine vehicles. (My evidence? Remember Professor Andrew Ford's 1992 study, *The Impact of Electric Vehicles on the Southern California Edison System*.) You'd save thousands of dollars.

But Arizona is hardly alone. Colorado offers both a $200 rebate when you buy an EV and a tax credit of 5 percent on the purchase price. Connecticut exempts you from sales tax. Louisiana gives you a tax credit equal to 2 percent of the purchase price. Utah gives one equal to 20 percent—with, however, a cap of $500, which seems to show that somebody in Utah is able to imagine EVs selling even cheaper than they do in Taiwan. There *is* an interesting EV company in West Valley City, Utah . . . .

Oklahoma offers a 10 percent credit, with a limit of $1,500. Pennsylvania offers the very modest bonus of no sales tax on the differential in price between an EV and its gasoline equivalent. If I am right that in a very few years EVs will be as cheap or cheaper than their combustion equivalents, that inducement will fade to nothing. EV-owners will still be eligible for Pennsylvania's other inducement, though: no registration fee at all.

What happy event will bring prices down so dramatically? Well, I think it will be a whole series of things. One, of course, is the simple fact of mass production. In 1992 Fiat was the world's largest producer of EVs (your Italian joke is coming true, *Road and Track*)— and the production run was 1,500. That's not very many to absorb the tooling-up expenses for a new car. When the run reaches, say, 15,000, the cost per car will drop dramatically. Say that in spades for the many little American companies that do conversions by hand.

Almost equally important will be the rapidly falling price and rapidly increasing power of EV batteries. For a hundred years now, batteries have been the one serious drawback of EVs. And for that same hundred years, inventors and scientists of all kinds have been looking for something better than the familiar lead-acids that Solo I had and Solo II still has. Even before the nineteenth century ended, a dozen new kinds of batteries had been invented. They did not come to much. In 1900 an electrical engineer named E. J. Wade gave a speech before the Institute of Electrical Engineers. In the course of it, he classified all the forms of storage batteries then in existence. Here is his complete list:

> Practical: Lead-sulfuric acid.
> Unpractical: All others.

Among those who set out to prove Wade wrong was Thomas Edison. Edison developed a nickel-iron battery, which he announced would soon be powering thousands of electric cars, and giving them splendid ranges. For one single electric car he was right, only that car happened to be fictional. In the year 1910 Tom Swift installed nickel-iron batteries in his electric runabout ("the fastest car on the road"), and with them won a 500-mile race. He beat dozens of gasoline cars. If nickel-iron batteries had really been that good, there probably would never have been a gasoline age.

But they weren't. They do have virtues, notably a 50 or 55 percent greater range than standard lead-acids. But they won't take a fast charge, they require a fair amount of maintenance, and they are very expensive. All these years later, they're still around—Chrysler has been trying them in a few of its overpriced electric vans just lately. But they do not seem to be a solution to the range problem of electric cars.

For most of the twentieth century there was no solution, and EVs languished. So did battery research, at least into the types of deep-discharge batteries that could power a car. Who cared? Gasoline was cheap, the world big, and pollution apparently no problem. As recently as 1950, there were only 53 million motor vehicles registered anywhere on Earth. Their emissions could float away with only modest effects on the atmosphere. Now there are well over 600 million registered vehicles, and by the end of the century there are likely to be a billion.* Even with catalytic converters, etc., it will be more than the planet can handle—if they all have combustion engines.

But help is on the way. EV help. What I think of as the First Environmental Age occurred between 1970 and 1980 (it was followed

---

*One footnote, just to show good faith. These figures come from *The End of the Road: The World Car Crisis and How We Can Solve It,* by Wolfgang Zuckermann (Chelsea Green, 1991), p. 22.

instantly by a dark age), and during it battery research resumed in earnest. During the last five years it has truly raced along, and it has had success. Wade's dictum no longer holds. All others are not impractical anymore—though most, I admit, are either too expensive or a long way from commercial production.

Right now people are working on zinc batteries, lithium batteries, sulfur-aluminum batteries, sodium batteries, nickel-metal-hydride batteries, and many others. The Advanced Battery Consortium, created a few years ago by the U.S. Department of Energy and the Big Three, has about a quarter of a billion to spend. As much or more is being spent abroad. And I don't just mean for lab tests. Zinc batteries, for example, are scheduled to go into production in a pilot plant in Austria a couple of years hence. The plant is to start with the capacity to produce enough batteries to equip 10,000 EVs a year. Sodium-sulfur batteries are being made in a small way right now by companies like Silent Power Ltd. in England. They have terrific range—and equally terrific maintenance problems.

Three new EV batteries, however, are already here and workable, or just about to be. First come the familiar nicads, or nickel-cadmium batteries, that people who care about recycling use in their flashlights. Nicads also come in much larger sizes, and they are currently the first and best answer to Wade. They are practical and they are available. Amtrak trains and subway cars have been equipped with them for years, and since 1992 so have a growing number of EVs.

I could go out and buy a set for Solo II tomorrow, and I would nearly double his range if I did. Since nicads are barely affected by cold weather, I would triple his winter range. And since they can take a couple of thousand rechargings, I could expect them to last for seven to ten years, and to take the car 120,000 miles or so.

There is, however, a drawback. A full set of batteries for Solo would cost me at least $16,000. No one is going to achieve parity with combustion cars *that* way.

But then, no one will have to. Mass production can cut battery costs just as effectively as it can cut car costs. Over the next two years, the French automobile company Peugeot expects to make thousands and perhaps tens of thousands of electric Peugeots and

Citroëns, and to power most of them with nicads. This huge order is the stimulus French and Germany battery makers have needed. Volume is headed up, and prices down. How far? Well, let me quote from a serious-looking pamphlet, "Les Cahiers de la Direction de la Communication de PSA Peugeot." What says the pamphlet? "Because they last several times longer, these batteries will cost about the same as lead-acid ones." Obviously Peugeot is comparing costs over the lifetime of an EV, not the initial price of any one set, nicad or lead-acid. But that's fair. It will very soon be the case that if you can afford an EV with ordinary lead batteries, you can afford one with nicads.

Nicads are here. The nickel-metal-hydride (NiMH) battery is almost here. This is the one to whose manufacturer the Advanced Battery Consortium gave its very first contract. From all reports, it's a dandy. It's supposed to give an even better range than you get with nicads—somewhere around 240 miles on level ground. No maintenance needed. Operating expenses less than half those of a combustion car. (This is true for nicads as well, according to a study done in 1992 by Renault.) Lifetime of the batteries: up to ten years. Probable cost of a set: $5,000.

But maybe the best thing about NiMH batteries is that they have lived in the real world. Lots of batteries look wonderful in the lab. So do some of the promising battery-substitutes, such as flywheel technology and fuel cells. Start using them, however, and you run into problems. This seems to have happened, for example, with the sodium-sulfur batteries that engineers at Ford developed, and that Ford had been planning to use in its electric Ecostars. The trouble is: Sodium-sulfur batteries work right only when their internal temperature is around 650°F. That's easy enough to arrange in the lab, a great deal harder in a battery attached to a moving car. Despite the limited production in both England and Sweden, it's beginning to look as if sodium-sulfur batteries have a very minor role to play in the future of electric cars.

No guarantee of success comes with NiMH batteries, either. None will be possible until they have proved themselves in repeated use, as nicads have. But they are not simply an untried idea. The

Ovonics Battery Company of Troy, Michigan, is the manufacturer. Energy Conversion Devices, also of Troy, is the parent company and developer. And the company has lots of real-world experience with NiMH batteries. It currently licenses nine battery manufacturers around the world to make small NiMH batteries for the portable electronics market. That fact enables me to feel a reasonable degree of confidence when I see quotes such as this one from Subhash Dhar, president of Ovonics: "The performance of electric cars is going to be so good we believe customers are not only going to buy them for pollution reasons but because they'll be high-performance cars."

That's two kinds of new batteries that are here, or almost here. What's the third? Lead-acid. The manufacturers of standard car batteries have not failed to notice the Advanced Battery Consortium, and the nicads and NiMH, and the zinc battery plant in Austria (which is partly owned in Boston). It has occurred to them that they could lose the whole EV market, maybe even the whole car market. So they have been doing some heavy-duty research of their own. Successfully. You might suppose that in the more than ninety years between E. J. Wade and now, lead-acids would have gone about as far as they could go. You'd be wrong.

"We think that lead-acid technology will probably get about twice as good in the next two years," says Bill Van Amburg of the organization called Calstart. That's just an opinion, though a highly informed one, Calstart being near the center of EV research. But the performance of the brand-new Horizon lead-acid battery is plain fact. Right now, this minute, a set of Horizon lead-acids would increase Solo's range by about 30 percent. It would cut his charging time to under an hour. And that's not even the final product. The forthcoming 1995 version of the Horizon would increase his range by 50 percent and still keep charging time under an hour. These advanced lead-acid batteries can be bought today, if you're in a position to get them through the Electric Power Research Institute.

If, like me, you're not, then you may have to wait a year, until the original pilot plant has been joined by two big automated factories. The price is then supposed to drop radically. Precise figure? I don't have one. But I do know that advanced lead-acids are going to have to compete with nicads and NiMH, and probably in a very few years with zinc batteries and flywheels, too. The price will not be exorbitant.

Enough about batteries. We were talking about why EVs will be able to sell at the same price as guzzlers, if not cheaper. There is one more reason besides the economies of mass production. Electric motors are easier to make than gasoline engines. (Incidentally, they're also more efficient. Solo's motor utilizes nearly 80 percent of the power the batteries send it. A typical gasoline engine utilizes about 20 percent of the energy in the gas.)

A gasoline engine has to handle constant explosions, high temperatures, corrosive wastes. An electric motor has to rotate.

Typically, the motor in an EV is a sealed unit that requires no maintenance at all for the first 100,000 miles. It requires no exhaust system, radiator, oil chamber, etc., etc. It needs no elaborate drive train—in some cases it needs none at all. There is one Japanese EV that has a small electric motor in each of the wheels—and each of the wheels can be turned 90 degrees. What *that* means is that the car can go sideways, thus enabling its owner to slip into parking places that even the most skilled parallel parker finds impossible.

All the EV needs is a smallish motor, a number of light electronic controls, brakes, and a set of good batteries. Make EVs in quantity, and of course they will be cheaper than comparable guzzlers.

But now there is another question to raise. Electric cars are no use at all without electricity. Back in Wyoming, I had assured Rod that there was plenty. Enough surplus generating capacity just in southern California to charge up half a million EVs a night.

If I had known then what I know now, I would have given Rod an even more impressive figure. It's actually a million EVs that could be charged nightly in southern California without Southern Cal Edison having to build any new plants for the purpose. Nationally, there's enough surplus generating power at night to keep somewhere between 20 and 40 million EVs on the road. Being conservative, I'll take the lower figure. Here is Gary Purcell of the Electric Power Research Institute speaking: "You could build 20 million electric vehicles like the Impact today—and not have to build any new power plants, because there's so much off-peak energy available."

It won't be clean energy, of course, except the small amount that comes from hydro, from wind systems, and from photovoltaics. And even they carry a price. The big West Coast wind farms are turning out to be very hard on hawks, large numbers of which get killed each year as they migrate. Most hydro projects flood good land, or give a mud bath to some pretty canyon. PV panels take a lot of energy to make. Personally, I think there *is* such a thing as free lunch, but I can't see that there's any free power for automobiles.

Clearly, however, some types are much more costly than others. And in terms of pollution, clearly electric power is one of the bargains. This is true even though nearly half the surplus generating capacity is in coal-fired plants. Granted, they are big polluters. All by themselves, coal-burning power plants produce nearly two-thirds of all the sulfur dioxide that pours into the North American air, and a generous share of the nitrogen oxide as well.

But an easy fix is at hand. A new system called natural gas reburn injects about 20 percent natural gas just above the main fires in a coal-burning plant—and these upper flames eliminate nearly all the nitrogen oxide and about 25 percent of the sulfur dioxide. Another new system called combined cycle generation reduces the amount of fossil fuel you have to burn—and thus the pollution—by half.

But it's when the electricity for EVs comes straight from natural gas–fired plants that the real bargain occurs. There is still what engineers call upstream pollution for the EV. But it is no greater than the upstream pollution for a gasoline car.

When people compare the two kinds of cars in an environmental way, they tend to think only about the emissions from the gasoline car as you drive it versus the emissions from the power plant for the EV as you charge it. That is an incomplete equation. Gasoline doesn't magically appear at the filling station with a pollution-free past. There has been pollution every step of the way: drilling for the oil, shipping it, refining it—which is a fairly filthy process—getting it to the service station, pumping it into your car.

For an EV powered by natural gas generators, the upstream pollution is the sum of that caused in drilling, shipping to the power plant, and burning. The two figures are almost identical. And the zero-emission of the EV is now 100 percent gain.

So far I have described the future of electric cars as if it were certain to happen just that way. I do think it is likely to. But it makes sense to consider some alternative scenarios.

1. Suppose the Big Three do succeed in getting the 2-5-10 requirement outlawed everywhere but California. In fact, let's suppose they are able to stop it even there. How much of an EV market will there be then? Obviously less than with the requirement. But probably not a lot less. The interest in EVs is a global phenomenon, like the pollution itself. If individual states are not allowed to require a gradual transition to EVs, my guess is that the federal government will require it—though probably not beginning as early as 1998. And if the big American automobile companies are not prepared to mass-market electric vehicles, plenty of foreign companies are. Peugeot, Citroën, Fiat, Renault, a whole host of Japanese and Korean firms are more than willing. There are also several U.S. firms, either new or new to the car business, rapidly gearing up to mass-produce EVs. The two I'm most aware of are Renaissance Cars in Florida and Taylor-Dunn in California. (You want details? Look in the epilogue.)

2. Suppose none of the batteries work out as well as I predict. Suppose that NiMH batteries never do yield a 240-mile range, zinc doesn't pan out, nicads stay expensive.

In that case, hybrid vehicles are going to have a bright future. Hybrids have both an electric motor and a small gasoline engine. In local driving they are wholly electric. Go on a long trip, and you shift to gasoline, quietly recharging your batteries as you roll along. Such cars already exist as prototypes. Volvo has the most interesting one I've heard about.

3. Suppose the new batteries do fine on range, are reasonably priced, but still take intolerably long to recharge. In that case, a lot of charging will shift from people's own garages to a network of quick-charge stations like the ones in La Rochelle. Nissan has already penciled out such a network for southern California. It in-

volves chargers about the size of small iceboxes—no way could you carry one in the car. You go to a filling station, just as owners of gasoline cars have been doing for ninety years. There you plug in for 15 minutes—unless you're in a real hurry. In that case, you stay only six minutes, and leave with half a charge. Say, enough for 75 or 100 miles.

The filling stations wouldn't have to be expensive, either. No huge buried tanks to hold the gasoline, no smoke-belching tank trucks supplying them. Something more like a money machine outside a bank. Slip your card in, get your juice, and be on your way.

There are ten service stations like that in Geneva, Switzerland, right now. Suppose there had been a national network of them in the United States in 1991. Suppose Nissan—or Mobil, or Pacific Gas and Electric—had one every thirty miles along Interstate 80, with maybe a few extra ones in places like Donner Pass. Even with my primitive lead-acids, I could have driven Solo home in a breeze.

The power companies are not entirely happy with such a scenario, because it involves a lot of daytime charging. It's only during the hours from 11 P.M. to 5 A.M. that they have so much surplus capacity. Charge during the day, and you're just adding to peak load.

What's my solution here? More solar panels, the perfect daytime charging system. More are coming, too. Solar panels, which I have gradually learned to call photovoltaic panels, or just PV, are still too expensive, but their use is spreading anyway.

Take, for example, the fifty electric-car parking places (equal to La Rochelle!) that are being installed next to rapid transit stations around Boston. Twenty-five of them, divided between Alewife and Braintree stations, will have PV panels. On nice sunny days the panels will both charge the parked EVs and feed the grid. On so-so days, they'll just charge the cars. And on miserable days they'll rest, and let the utility handle peak load unaided.

But it's seldom bad weather all over the United States, or even all over one region. As more and more photovoltaic charging stations get built, the assurance of help every day with peak load will grow.

PV charging stations in cities have one more advantage, an unexpected one. Sheila Lynch, the Boston consultant who designed the city's EV parking set-up, discovered it just last year. Everybody hates smog. One reason for turning to electric vehicles in the first place is to minimize the production of smog in cities like Boston and Los Angeles. But photovoltaic panels actually work better—produce more electricity—when smog levels are high. So the worse the air is where you live, the more you are helped by PV. That goes a fair distance toward compensating for the present high cost. Once that cost begins to drop, all our cities will have cool, shady parking places, reserved for electric cars, and the shade will be created by solar panels, busy making pollution-free electricity.

4. Suppose EVs turn out not to be the best kind of alternative vehicle. There are also propane-powered cars, cars that run on ethanol and methanol, cars that use natural gas. What if one of them proves environmentally superior?

Me: It won't happen. The other alternatives all require combustion engines.

Skeptic: Yes, and most EVs depend on big, dirty power plants. Answer the question. What if EVs turn out not to be the best choice?

Me: Well, in that case I think we'll be seeing a lot of vehicles that run on natural gas. Pick the right spot, and you can see quite a few now.

Go to Texas. In 1990 the Texas legislature passed a law almost as radical as California's 2-5-10. It said that starting in 1991 "no vehicle may be purchased or leased by a municipal authority . . . that cannot use natural gas as the fuel source." The law just requires capability, not actual use, but use is coming on fast. Houston, for example, is busy converting all 1,500 buses in the city transit system to liquefied natural gas. A good move. The improvement in air quality is substantial. I'm for it.

But sometime in the twenty-first century we'll run short on natural gas, whether to power buses or to feed generating plants. When that happens, there'd better be a lot of PV waiting to serve a lot of EVs. I think natural gas vehicles are a fine way to buy time. I also think we'd better use that time to get Donner Pass wired up, batteries radically improved, fuel cells developed, photovoltaics made cheap and easy. We might even think about redesigning our society so that people don't have to drive quite so much.

5. What if gasoline stages an environmental comeback? It could, you know. If auto makers can get the number of miles per gallon up high enough, pollution per vehicle would drop to a tiny fraction of the present figure. And perhaps they can. I have seen plans for a car that gets 300 miles to the gallon, a car that you could drive coast-to-coast on one tank of gasoline. It's no pipe dream, either, but a carefully thought-out project of Amory Lovins at the Rocky Mountain Institute. Suppose such cars get built. *Then* what happens to EVs?

Answer: They're still around. In fact, they're what gets built. Lovins's "supercar" is actually a very light hybrid, weighing just under 1,000 pounds. Being made of carbon-fiber, it's as safe or safer than steel cars weighing three times as much.

The supercar will have very little air resistance, mostly because the underside will be as smooth as the top. It will have very little road resistance, because it runs on EV tires. It will produce very little waste energy because it has a very small engine that always runs at the same maximally efficient speed.

How is that possible? To give an answer, I need to glance first at the engines in most current American cars. They're huge. They can put out 100 to 200 horsepower. They're so big that they use only about a sixth of their full strength when you're cruising on a freeway. More like a twentieth when you go down a city street. So what's all that extra power for? Fast starts. Lightning acceleration. The American power thrill.

Lovins's car permits fast acceleration, too, but by an entirely different method. As you drive one of these 300-mile-to-the-gallon cars, its tiny gasoline engine (10 or 20 horsepower) is doing two things simultaneously. It's powering the two small electric motors that turn the drive wheels. And it's storing whatever surplus power it makes in a small battery bank. There might be four batteries.

Now you come up behind a truck you want to pass. You floor the accelerator. You zoom by. Your little gas engine has continued to run steadily at its ideal speed—but now the batteries join it, and you have plenty of power for passing. Once you've gone whizzing by— or shot up a hill, or gunned out of a ditch—the electric motors no longer need extra amps, and they cease to draw on the batteries. These now come back to full charge, fed either by the little engine or by the regenerative braking that is an integral part of the design.

Lovins is dead serious. The Rocky Mountain Institute is talking with potential manufacturers right now. The plan is for supercars to be on the road three to six years from now—though ones you might buy in 1998 or 1999 would be an early version that gets "only" 150 miles to the gallon. That's adequate, even for people like me, who wish we didn't import one drop of oil from anywhere. If I'm not satisfied with the batteries available when it's time to buy Solo III, I may get one myself.

Now, there is one last matter to bring up. Earlier in this chapter I claimed that conventional cars will not be subsidizing EVs. It'll be the other way round, I said. By this I do not mean that a few years hence GM will be building nice little EVs for $9,000 but actually selling them for $10,000, and using the extra money to cut the price of Oldsmobiles. I'm talking about pollution costs. You may remember that John Moffet said that in terms of pollution a current standard car costs society 4 to 8 cents a mile. Andrew Ford said a current standard car costs society about $8,000 during its life.

How do these costs show up? Most directly as many-sided attempts to clean the air—or the beaches where a tanker has crashed, or the soil under an old filling station. But there's also a complex array of health costs, prevention costs, transportation costs.

Being zero-emission, EVs have very low pollution costs per mile. When you add in their upstream pollution, you still get a figure of perhaps 2 cents. In short, EVs can and do provide the relatively clean air that conventional cars come along to pollute, and thus they subsidize the guzzlers.

Two cents of pollution per mile is still too much. A mule at 0 cents would be better, if not very practical for longer trips. A supercar at half a cent a mile would also be better. Solo at maybe a tenth of a cent a mile is better right now. I guess less driving, though wildly unlikely, would be best of all. It's too nice a planet to spoil.

HOW TO GET ONE

Noel, I have 49 years in battery manufacturing, design, and engineering. I also have some battery patents. I can tell you it will take at least three years of research before you can write even a brief picture of the EV business from a technical standpoint.
—FRED DANIEL, *product manager, Trojan Battery Company, October 10, 1991*

I CAN'T END THIS book without saying a few words directly to potential buyers of electric cars, and even giving them some addresses. Obviously I have no technical standing at all, even after three years. But I do have some phone numbers—and some opinions.

The first is that if you get an electric car to commute in (and for another year or two you'd be crazy to get one for any other purpose), get one with the longest range you can find. Do not for a minute think that because you're only going to drive sixteen miles to work and sixteen miles home, a range of fifty miles is all you could possibly want, and more. It's barely enough. For several years to come, all but the best EVs will have standard lead-acid batteries. Cars thus powered *can* be driven regularly down to red bar, but it takes a lot out of them. Their batteries live strenuously and die young. Far better, when you can, to stay in the upper half of the charge.

Even when nickel-cadmium batteries become affordable, this will hold true. Unlike the little nickel-cadmium dry cells you get for flashlights and radios, nickel-cadmium car batteries have no memories and do not need deep discharges. Nicads last a long time. They last even longer when not pushed to their limits.

My second piece of advice is also about range. Whatever the manufacturer tells you it is, in your mind cut that figure in half. Not because the manufacturer is hyping you, but because every trip is in

211

the end a round trip. All but that first one home from the factory, anyway.

I realized that half-range is what counts about a week after I got back from California. Friends who live thirty miles away had invited Anne and me to dinner. Their nine-year-old son Philip is deeply interested in electric cars. They naturally assumed that we'd come in Solo, and that Phil would get his first ride in an EV. But we took Anne's car. Not because we were indifferent to the boy's hopes, or afraid of the dark. Our fear was getting stranded. With Solo I's forty-mile range in hill country, we'd have no trouble getting there. But would he recharge enough during a three- or at most four-hour visit to take us all the way home? Especially if I had him out while we were there, giving Phil a ride? I was unwilling to find out.

My third and last piece of advice is to take advantage of some of the very large number of information sources there are in this country. Many are formidable, technical, and dull. But others are quite readable. I'm thinking, for example, of a magazine called *Home Power*. I never heard of it until Sue (of Sue and Dean's solar house) happened casually to mention it, well after I got my own photovoltaic system. When she showed me a copy, I subscribed as fast as I could get to my checkbook.

Home Power has rapidly become one of my two or three favorite magazines—and the only one I save back copies of. Suppose you were interested in Sun Frost refrigerators. *Consumer Reports* does not evaluate them—their market share is too small. *Home Power* does. Not only that, if a couple of New England subscribers to the magazine happen to be in Arcata, California, where Sun Frosts are made, they go right to the plant and interview the man who founded the company. Then they write up the interview and send it to *Home Power*, which prints it. Good interview, too.

The whole magazine has this kind of informal, we're-among-friends feel, though that does not prevent the editors from doing rigorous tests. They published the only consumer report on different makes of solar panels that I've ever seen. (My Solarex panels came out nicely.)

Electric cars used not to be at the center of the magazine's interest. Photovoltaics, wind generators, and small hydro occupied that spot. But early in 1993 EVs moved right on into the center, and now get as much attention as phantom loads on household appliances or overshot waterwheels. Fifteen dollars for a year's subscription to *Home Power* is as good a bargain as the French rolls at the Cleveland Museum of Art.

Even a last note has to end. This one will conclude with a group of addresses.

Some current makers of EVs for sale in the United States

BAT International, 2471 S., 2570 W., West Valley City, UT 84119. 801-977-0119. Sells a commuter model (batteries in the truck bed) converted Ford Ranger pickup for $24,100, and a utility model (batteries under the bed) for $25,600. Both have a top speed of 70, and a range of 50–80 miles. BAT also sells a converted Geo Metro for $15,900. Top speed: 75. Range: 50–80 miles. BAT uses a somewhat controversial catalyst in the lead-acid batteries. On the whole, western EV-owners seem to believe in it, and eastern ones tend to be skeptical.

Beetles Unlimited, 19804 Aurora Ave. N., Seattle, WA 98133. 206-546-1803. As the name suggests, they convert only VW Beetles. Top speed: 73. Range: 45–70 miles. Price: $15,495 to $17,495, depending on which year Beetle they have converted (and re-conditioned).

Incidentally, VW itself is planning to revive a slightly enlarged Beetle (they had one at the 1994 Detroit Auto Show), and there is a rumor that it will be available as an electric. A year or two hence.

Burckhardt Turbines, 1258 N. Main St., Unit B2B, Fort Bragg, CA 95437. 707-961-0459. If you supply the vehicle, Burckhardt will do a no-frills conversion for $8,500. If they supply it, prices are $12,000 and up. Burckhardt also sells reconditioned secondhand EVs. Prices for *them* start at $7,500. Top speed: 65. Range: 40–60 miles, depending, as is the case with all EVs, "on terrain, number of stops, driving technique, and battery age."

California Electric Cars, 1669 Del Monte Blvd., Seaside, CA 93955. 408-899-2012. Sells converted pickup trucks and light utility vehicles with a range of 60 miles at highway speeds, and up to 100 miles in city driving. Price: $19,500. They also make a two-seater sports car for which they claim a range of 140 miles. Price: $30,000.

Domino Cars, 102 New Haven, Milford, CT 06460. 203-877-0076. Sells an EV called the Minilight, which weighs only about 1,500 pounds. Top speed: 75. Range: 65–90 miles. Price: $21,000.

Eco-Motion, 6021 32nd Ave. NE, Seattle, WA 98115. 206-524-1351. Sells a racy-looking two-seater with twenty lead-acid batteries. Top speed: 70. Range: 50–80 miles. Price: $15,995.

Electric Motor Cars, 4301 Kingfisher, Houston, TX 77035. 713-729-8668. Will convert almost any small or mid-size vehicle, including some with four-wheel drive. Customer supplies the vehicle. The range is 50–70 miles for most conversions, but Geos and Festivas get closer to 80. Prices range from $6,000 up to as much as $30,000, depending on how fancy a job you want, and whether you need air conditioning, regnerative braking, etc.

Electric Vehicles of America, P.O. Box 59, Maynard, MA 01754. 508-897-9393. Does high-class pickup conversions (you supply the vehicle) for $13,000. Top speed: 70. Level ground range: 100 miles. Range on continuous 2 percent grade: 60–80 miles.

Herb Adams V.S.E., 23865 Fairfield, Carmel, CA 93923. 408-649-8423. Sells converted VW Rabbits for $19,000. Top speed: 70. Range: 60–110 miles.

MendoMotive, 30151 Navarro Ridge Rd., Albion, CA 95410. 707-937-3136. Specializes in conversions and in tractors (lawn and real). Bring your own vehicle, and they'll convert for somewhere between $9,000 and $12,000. They also sell an electric replica of a 1955 Porsche for $30,000. Range for all: 40–60 miles. Top speed: 65. The tractors come slightly used from Japan, and are converted by MendoMotive. A big one will cost you $9,000 or even $10,000. Current sales are mostly in Central America.

All these machines can also be ordered through Real Goods, 966 Mazzoni St., Ukiah, CA 95482. 707-468-9292.

Renaissance Cars, 2300 Commerce Park Drive, Palm Bay, FL 32905. 407-676-2228. This is the second American company in recent times to build an EV from the ground up. Renaissance will make a two-seater called the Tropica. It has a molded plastic body on an aluminum frame, and thus is light enough to need only twelve batteries. The car is scheduled to go on sale in the summer of 1994, but will initially be available only in Florida and California. Price: $10,850. (Are you listening, Chrysler?) Range: 50–80 miles. Top speed: 60.

In case you're wondering what the first company is, it's Taylor-Dunn of Anaheim, California, which has just finished selling 400 light electric trucks to a company in Mexico City. Taylor-Dunn also sells EVs in England and in South America. But their EVs are not available in the U.S., because they are not yet certified for street use. Here, that is. They are certified in the U.K., Brazil, Chile, and Argentina.

Sebring Auto-Cycle, P.O. Box 1479, Sebring, FL 33871. 813-471-0424. Sells the ZEV-Colt. Top speed: 60. Range: 40–60 miles. Price: $24,000.

Solar Car, 1300 Lake Washington Road, Melbourne, FL 32935. 407-254-2997. Solar Car will convert a customer's pickup for $14,000. The customer gets an EV with a range of 55–80 miles, and a top speed of 65. (And possibly more. I know a customer or two who have had them up to 75). Solar Car also sells conversion kits. Price: $6,975.

Solectria, 27 Jason Street, Arlington, MA 02174. 508-658-2231. Solectria is probably the highest-tech company now making EVs. All their cars and pickups have brushless AC drive systems, and all offer regenerative braking. All have electric heaters that put out plenty of heat. There are currently two major EV car races in this country, and Solectria routinely wins them both.

Not surprisingly, Solectria is also one of the more expensive companies. Their four-passenger car costs $26,050. It provides a 60-mile range (at 50 mph—you get more if you're driving slower) and a top speed of 60. The two-passenger model costs $28,280, and has a 70-mile range. The same model with nickel-cadmium batteries costs $59,350, has a top speed of 70, and a range of 120 miles. Pickups run around $43,000.

U.S. Electricar, 117 Morris Street, Sebastopol, CA 95472. 707-829-4545. This is the firm I knew as Solar Electric Engineering. The company has moved, changed its name, and increased in size by a factor of about ten since I went out to pick up Solo in 1991.

The company has also gotten a lot more high-tech and a lot more expensive. It is to the West Coast what Solectria is to the East.

U.S. Electricar now sells brand-new converted Geo Prisms for $39,000, and brand-new converted Chevy pickups for the same $43,000 price as Solectria. What, besides a new vehicle, do you get that I didn't get for $17,500? Well, first you get the same kind of acceleration and speed that gasoline cars have: 0–60 in 12 seconds, top speed 85. You get the same new charging system that GM Impacts have—absolutely foolproof, works even during a hard rain, will charge from either a 110 or a 220 outlet. And you get modestly improved range: 50–80 miles with the Prisms, 50–90 with the pickups.

Vermont Electric Car Co., RD 3, Box 3272, Middlesex, VT 05602. 802-229-2533. Converts Chevy S-10 trucks. (You supply truck.) Price: $17,900. Top Speed: 65. Range, even in hilly Vermont: 75 miles. These trucks have a 120-volt system, using 20 batteries.

VoltAge, Inc., 18422 South Broadway, Gardena, CA 90248. 310-532-4536. Produces a car called the Voltsvagon. Top speed: 65. Range: 30–45 miles. Price: $11,500.

Author's warning: I have not test-driven even one of these vehicles. Most of the data comes from the companies themselves, and the rest is from the *1994 Buyer's Guide to Electric Vehicles* by Philip Terpstra. I believe it to be accurate, but guarantee nothing. I don't even guarantee that every single company will still be in business when this book comes out, though I surely hope it.

Electric car dealers
So far as I know, there are currently only two EV dealers in the United States—though if Renaissance Cars takes off, there will be lots more very soon. They are:

Green Motorworks, 5228 Vineland Avenue, North Hollywood, CA 91601. 818-766-3800. Green Motorworks stocks an import: the little Danish EV called the Kewet. Despite Robert Mohr's taking one around the world, it's basically a city car. Top speed: 45. Range: 35–

45 miles. (Yes, I know Mohr got 50, sometimes even 60. He must be a gifted driver. The dealers claim only 45.) Price: $12,900.

Green Motorworks usually has somewhere between five and ten other EVs in stock. Unlike the purpose-built Kewet, these are all conversions of gasoline cars. Prices range from $10,000 up into the twenties.

Cart-Aways, 16 Waites Wharf, Newport, RI 02840. 401-849-0010. Don Crockett, who runs Cart-Aways, is the eastern dealer for Kewets. Price in Rhode Island: $13,500.

Electric vehicle associations

The biggest group, the AAA of electric cars, is the Electric Auto Association, 2710 St. Giles Lane, Mountain View, CA 94040. The EAA has chapters in Arizona, Florida, Indiana, Maryland, Massachusetts, Nevada, New Jersey, New Mexico, North Carolina, Ohio, Texas, Utah, Washington state, Washington, D.C., and Canada, as well as ten chapters in California. You can get a sample copy of the EAA newsletter by sending them a stamped, self-addressed envelope.

Publications

Current EVents, same address as the Electric Auto Association.

Home Power, P.O. Box 520, Ashland, OR 97520.

1994 Buyer's Guide to Electric Vehicles, P.O. Box 7093, Kamuela, HI 96743.